Britisl Midland Airways

CHARLES WOODLEY

AIRLINES SERIES, VOLUME 3

Front cover image: Boeing 707 G-BMAZ was one of the few examples to carry the full British Midland Livery. (Rob Hodgkins)

Contents page image: Boeing 737 srs 300 G-OBMH at Glasgow in April 1992. (Eric Melrose)

Published by Key Books
An imprint of Key Publishing Ltd
PO Box 100
Stamford
Lincs PE19 1XQ

www.keypublishing.com

The right of Charles Woodley to be identified as the author of this book has been asserted in accordance with the Copyright, Designs and Patents Act 1988 Sections 77 and 78.

ISBN 978 1 802820 36 2

Typeset by SJmagic DESIGN SERVICES, India.

Acknowledgments

Many people have helped me in the preparation of this book, either by supplying or permitting the use of images or written material or by providing encouragement. Thanks go to: Eric Melrose, Kerry Taylor, Rob Hodgkins, Denis Deparis, Dave Welch, Graham Marchbank, the staff at *Derby Telegraph*/BPM Media, Jerry Hughes, Lewis Grant, David Whitworth, Trevor Hall, Michael Bajcar, H J Black, Gerry Hill, Roy G Plant, Barry Friend, Glyn Charles Jones, Kev Colbran, Ioan Reed-Aspley at East Midlands Airport, Malcolm Ginsberg at *Business Travel News*, Chris Adams at Reach plc, Brian Jones, Graham Ward, Ralf Mantufel, Charlie Stewart, and Anita Baker at Key Publishing.

If I have inadvertently omitted anyone, please accept my apologies and thanks.

Contents

Introduction

B ritish Midland Airways was a survivor. For over 70 years, under various identities, the company steadily grew from a flying school into a major UK scheduled airline that outlasted more flamboyant contemporaries such as British Eagle, Dan-Air and British Caledonian Airways, eventually operating wide-bodied Airbus aircraft. As Derby Airways, the company built up a network of scheduled services and holiday charter flights from the Midlands. Its takeover of the assets of the ailing Mercury Airlines in 1964 brought it not only useful check-in and office space at Manchester Airport but also the services of 24-year-old Michael Bishop, who was to rapidly rise through the ranks to the very top of the airline.

Under his leadership, and with a new identity as British Midland Airways, the company introduced many innovations. Boeing 707 jets were acquired for transatlantic charter flights, and when these operations ran up against bureaucratic obstacles, the aircraft were used to start up the 'instant airline' concept, being hired out with or without support packages to airlines in developing countries anxious to join the 'big-jet' league.

Realising the futility of trying to compete head-on with British Airways at that stage, the carrier found ways to co-operate with the national carrier, expanding its route network through a series of route-swap arrangements. Eventually, British Midland felt confident enough to apply for licences to compete directly on domestic trunk routes out of its new primary operating base at Heathrow, and later to Amsterdam, taking on KLM as well as British Airways. These licences were granted and successfully operated, but another ambition, to open scheduled transatlantic services out of London, remained unfulfilled, so, instead, the airline successfully applied for permission to operate to Washington DC and Chicago from Manchester.

Over the years, several revamps ensured that the carrier's image remained fresh. The most dramatic of these in 2001 saw the adoption of a new name, the somewhat enigmatic 'bmi'. The mid-2000s saw the development of the long-haul network eastward, with new routes to the Middle East and India. In 2007, bmi took over the struggling medium-haul airline BMed, and the acquisition of a major shareholding in bmi by Lufthansa in 2009 brought about membership of the Star Alliance airline conglomerate. Bmi was now in the 'big league', but, like many carriers, was struggling to break even. Lufthansa instigated a restructuring of its subsidiary but failed to find a way out of its financial problems. Bmi was put up for sale, and, at the end of 2011, it was purchased by the owners of British Airways. Integration of its services followed, and the final flight under the bmi name landed at Heathrow in October 2012.

Chapter 1
The Beginning

During the 1930s, towns and cities throughout the UK were busy establishing their own municipal flying grounds. These were seen as a symbol of a progressive town council, and, in April 1938, Derby Corporation were looking for an enterprising individual or commercial undertaking to run the airport they were in the process of constructing and setting up at Burnaston, six miles south-west of their city. The job went to Captain Roy Harben DFC, who secured a lease on the land at Burnaston, and, assisted by E W Philips, successfully tendered for an Air Ministry contract to train pilots for the RAF Volunteer Reserve, setting up Air Schools Ltd for this purpose. The flying school became operational in the autumn of 1938, although the aerodrome was not to have its official opening ceremony until the following June. The Derby Aero Club was also set up to provide flying facilities for individuals with fairly deep pockets, but with the coming of World War Two, Air Schools focused its energies on the training of pilots for the RAF at Burnaston and at an outstation at Wolverhampton airfield. Throughout the war, large fleets of de Havilland 82A Tiger Moths and Miles Magister monoplanes were employed for this purpose. On 17 June 1939, the flying field at Burnaston finally had its official opening as the municipal airport for Derby. The end of the war in 1945 brought about the abrupt cancellation of the large military contracts, but Air Schools Ltd was fortunate enough to secure further, smaller, contracts for the training of pilots and navigators for the RAF Volunteer Reserve, using twin-engined Avro Ansons and, in later years, Percival Prentice trainers. In 1946, Air Schools Ltd set up a parent company, Derby Aviation, to manage its efforts to diversify into civil air transport. Light aircraft were acquired for the flying clubs set up at Burnaston and Wolverhampton, and these were also available for charter flights whenever such work could be found. On 21 August 1947, Captain Bill Wooden carried out Derby Aviation's first such charter, transporting three motorcycling enthusiasts from Derby to the Isle of Man

Derby Airways' first DH89A Dragon Rapide G-AIUK at Burnaston. (Roy G Plant)

Derby Airways' first Dakota G-ANTD taxies in at Bournemouth in July 1959. (Jerry Hughes)

Derby Airways' first Dakota G-ANTD awaits its passengers at Bournemouth in July 1959. (Jerry Hughes)

and back in Miles Messenger G-AILL for that year's TT races. After the sudden death of Roy Harben in February 1947, Ron Paine, the Chief Engineer at Wolverhampton, was brought across to Burnaston to strengthen the group management team. In 1948, the company bought out Reeves and Kenning, an organisation which had among its assets an aircraft furnishing department and a small air charter division. This move added eight-seater DH 89A Dragon Rapide biplane G-AIUK to the fleet. A second Rapide, G-AKOV, was acquired in August 1950 and these aircraft were also utilised on contracts for army co-operation work. This included acting as aerial 'targets' for searchlight crews under training. By 1952, the organisation had grown to encompass a staff of 55, an aircraft fleet comprising two Rapides, a Miles Messenger and a twin-engined Miles Gemini, and Air Registration Board-approved engineering bases at Derby and Wolverhampton. During that year, the aircraft flew some 46,000 revenue-miles. Diversification became more necessary as the Air Ministry contracts came to an end and the RAF Volunteer Reserve flying schools were wound down and finally closed in 1954, and so an application for a licence for Derby Aviation's first scheduled passenger service was submitted to the authorities. This covered flights between the Midlands and the Channel Islands, and, following approval, the first service took off on 18 July 1953, with Captain E W Lines in command of Rapide G-AEAL. The aircraft flew from Derby and Wolverhampton to Jersey via a stop at Birmingham to clear customs formalities, and on many of the early services Captain Lines' wife, Audrey, acted as the stewardess. The Jersey service was seasonal, being suspended at the end of September 1953. By then, the company had carried 573 passengers out of Wolverhampton and 634 out of Derby, producing a healthy 75 per cent load factor.

The success of the first season prompted a look at larger aircraft with an eye on traffic growth in the future. At that time, the market was flooded with RAF-surplus Douglas Dakota aircraft available at rock-bottom prices, and so it was almost inevitable that Derby Aviation would acquire an example. Flown into Burnaston by Captain Lines on 16 April 1955, it underwent conversion to airline standards and civilian registration as G-ANTD. It also acquired a name, 'Dovedale', beginning a tradition of naming the aircraft in the company's fleet after the Derbyshire dales. Its first commercial operation took the form of a ship's crew charter flight from Manchester to Amsterdam on 3 May 1955, and, three days later, it began working the scheduled service linking Wolverhampton and Derby to Jersey. The airline was also able to pick up some useful additional revenue from the end of that month. A nationwide UK rail strike crippled the distribution of daily newspapers and Derby Aviation was among the independent airlines contracted to replace the trains in this work. From then until 15 June 1955, the company transported 84,000 newspapers each night from Blackbushe Airport in Hampshire to Cardiff and Exeter. During 1955, Derby Aviation utilised its engineering resources and expertise to convert ten Mosquito PR35 aircraft for aerial survey duties in Canada with Spartan Air Services. The company also used Avro Anson G-AMDA for geological survey work in conjunction with Canadian Aero Services, flying the aircraft around the UK at 1,800ft and recording variations in the earth's magnetic field.

Derby Airways acquired its first Dakota in 1955. G-AMSX, seen here at Southampton in May 1962, came from Cambrian Airways. (Barry Friend collection)

Chapter 2

Building a Network

B y the end of 1955, all but one of the company's Rapides had been disposed of. Business was booming, the Dakota was fully utilised, and more aircraft were needed if expansion was to continue. News was received that the West African Airways Corporation had placed its fleet of four-engined Miles Marathon airliners on the market at a very modest price, and Ron Paine was despatched to Lagos to inspect them. This resulted in a deal to purchase two examples, which were ferried to Burnaston. Although British-built, these particular aircraft still required conversion work to meet UK airworthiness standards, and this was to prove a major challenge for the company's engineers. The wing spars needed modification and the fuselage bulkheads needed to be relocated further aft, in the process increasing their passenger capacity from 18 to 20. Their nosewheel frames were strengthened to cope with operations from the bumpy grass runway surface at Burnaston, and the Marathons were completely rewired. Even after all this work, the aircraft entered service with many areas still in need of improvement. No autopilots were fitted, the aircraft were unheated and had no toilets, and the passenger cabins and cockpits leaked whenever rain was encountered. The two Marathons, now registered as G-AMGW and G-AMHR and bearing the names 'Millers Dale' and 'Monsal Dale', were initially placed into service on the Jersey flights, and, in 1956, they were used, along with the Dakota, to open new routes to the Channel Islands from Oxford, Cambridge, Gloucester/ Cheltenham (Staverton) and Northampton (Sywell) airfields, and from Derby to Ostend. However, it was not just the aircraft that were under-equipped. Many of these airfields lacked hard runways,

Four Derby Airways Dakotas on the grass at Burnaston in 1963. (Dave Welch)

Four Derby Airways Dakotas at Burnaston in 1963. G-ANTD is nearest to the camera. (Dave Welch)

An aerial view of the Burnaston base, with two Dakotas and a Miles Marathon on the apron. (Derby Telegraph/ BPM Media)

and Burnaston had no control tower or radio beacon, no night lighting apart from flares and, like many of the airline's airports, no customs clearance facilities. The Derby–Ostend services had to call in at Birmingham for this purpose, and most Channel Island flights had to land at Bournemouth en route to complete these formalities. Early in 1956, a second Dakota had joined the Derby Aviation fleet, this one with a pedigree. On 24 February, G-AOGZ was flown by Captain Lines into Burnaston from RAF Silloth, where it had been civilianised after having served during World War Two as the personal transport of Field Marshall Bernard Montgomery. At the end of the 1956 summer season, some rationalisation of the airline's operations took place. The services out of Wolverhampton and Nottingham were dropped and all activity was concentrated on Derby. Before 1956 ended, Derby Aviation was involved in a humanitarian airlift. A failed uprising against communist rule in Hungary had resulted in refugees fleeing across the border into Austria. As part of an operation to bring many of them to the UK, the airline's two Dakotas carried out 18 round trips from Blackbushe Airport to Linz and Vienna during November 1956, transporting blankets and relief supplies on the outbound legs and bringing back over 600 refugees.

In 1957, Derby Aviation began a fruitful association with the aero engine division of Rolls-Royce. This company had manufacturing facilities close to both Derby and Glasgow and its personnel frequently travelled between the two locations. On 22 March 1957, the airline opened a new Derby–Glasgow route, encouraged by an arrangement whereby Rolls-Royce guaranteed to purchase 16 seats on each day's flights during the first year of the service; this commitment gradually reducing to zero over five years. The engine manufacturer also chartered Derby Aviation's Dakotas to transport aero engines, parts and technicians to customers throughout the world. Rolls-Royce Dart turbo-prop

Miles Marathon G-AMHR at Bournemouth in July 1959. (Jerry Hughes)

G-AMHR from another angle in July 1959. (Jerry Hughes)

engines were shipped to RAF bases throughout the Middle East and the Indian sub-continent, and 254 Avon turbo-jet engines were flown out to Sud Aviation in Toulouse for installation in the new Caravelle airliner. By the end of 1960, Derby Aviation had completed 100 of these flights. During 1957, the airline's engineers installed the Instrument Landing System in the Marathon aircraft. This proved useful for landing at many airports, but not so at Burnaston, which lacked the necessary complementary ground equipment. On 18 May 1957, Derby Aviation commenced flying on its first inclusive-tour contract for Dakota flights between Birmingham and Palma on behalf of Midland Air Tour Operators. In January of the following year, the airline began operating night flights for winter sports enthusiasts, departing Manchester late on Friday nights for Munich via Brussels, arriving in Munich at 0600hrs on Saturday. After a day's rest there, the same crew brought the aircraft back, taking off at midnight. During the spring of 1958, a boardroom decision was taken to rename the operating element of the airline as Derby Airways. From then onwards, as each aircraft went through the hangar for maintenance it re-emerged with Derby Airways titling. The change became official on 12 March 1959 when Derby Airways was registered as an airline company. A third Marathon joined the fleet in time for the summer 1958 season, during which the airline's three Dakotas flew to warmer climes, operating inclusive-tour flights out of Derby to Majorca, the Costa Brava, Italy and France. They were also utilised on 'fly-cruise' packages in conjunction with Royal Mail Lines. Holidaymakers sailed on this company's steamships to Miramar in Spain via Vigo (Spain) and Leixos (Portugal). After five nights ashore, they flew home, all for a total price of 32 guineas (£33.60). The hard-working Dakotas were also utilised on eight-day pilgrimage tours to the shrine at Lourdes. In mid-1958, Derby Airways announced that during the following year it would be leasing the prototype Handley Page Dart Herald

Above and below: Derby Airways Miles Marathon G-AMHR at Bournemouth in July 1959. (Jerry Hughes)

airliner G-AODE from the manufacturer, thus becoming the first operator of the type. Unfortunately, before this plan could take effect, the aircraft suffered a catastrophic engine fire when en route to the 1958 Farnborough Airshow and was written off in the ensuing forced landing. It was to be 1965 before the company eventually operated its first Herald.

On 8 April 1959, Derby Airways re-opened the route, which had previously been operated by the Welsh airline Cambrian Airways, from Staverton airfield, near Cheltenham, to the Channel Islands. This company was experiencing financial difficulties at the time, and, later that month, Derby Airways took on two of its Dakota aircraft, bringing the fleet up to five. During the course of that year, these machines were fitted out with the Decca Mk 8 navigation aid. This could be used in conjunction with a Decca letdown chart when landing at Burnaston in difficult weather conditions. Operations at the airport had also been made easier for passengers from March 1959 when customs facilities had become operational there in a new purpose-built customs hall. In 1959, Derby Airways became the first airline to operate scheduled services out of Luton airport, initially serving Jersey and, later, Dublin via Derby. The shortcomings of Burnaston as an airport had been apparent for some time, and, on 8 October 1959, Derby Town Council announced that the former RAF airfield at Castle Donington was to be developed into a new East Midlands Airport. Four other local authorities would later join with the council in the formation of a consortium for this purpose. Until the new airport was opened, Burnaston would have to suffice. Two days after this announcement, Derby Airways operated its first Winter Sunshine Cruise in conjunction with the Lord Bros tour company. On each of these two-week trips, a specially configured Dakota, with four seats removed to make space for a table in the cabin, departed Birmingham on a Saturday morning. After stops at Gatwick and Jersey to pick up passengers and a refuelling stop at Biarritz, the Dakota arrived at Madrid. After a two-day stopover there, it transported its passengers to Marrakesh for another two-night stay. Then it was on to Tenerife via a technical stop at Agadir. The passengers had a full week at leisure in Tenerife before proceeding onwards to Tangier for a two-night stopover, before finally flying back to the UK. For the 1960 summer season, the airline had six Dakotas in service, enabling the inclusive-tour programme to be expanded to include flights out of Cardiff and Bristol to Palma, Perpignan, Luxembourg and Ostend, and from Gatwick to Calvi and Dinard as well as Spain. The era of the Miles Marathons came to an end on 26 September 1960, when G-AMEW operated the airline's final services with the type, routeing Derby–Dublin–Derby–Luton–Derby. During the following lean winter months, Derby Airways was able to gain additional revenue from the operation of freight services for the state airline, British European Airways. From 2 February 1961, Dakotas flew nightly between Heathrow and Amsterdam on a contract that was extended well into the summer months. In July 1961, Derby Airways carried its one-millionth passenger.

For some time, the company had been looking for larger, four-engined and pressurised aircraft with which to expand its inclusive-tour route network. The ideal type seemed to be the Douglas DC-6A. This was a comparatively expensive aircraft to purchase, but plans were made to acquire two used examples from American Airlines and ferry them to the UK. Before these plans could be proceeded with, however, the UK independent airline Overseas Aviation (CI) Ltd went bankrupt and its controlling bank, Lombards, advertised its five Canadair Argonaut aircraft for sale at a very modest price. In a move that would later be seen as hasty, Derby Airlines entered into a deal to purchase the aircraft; the arrangement also contained for a provision for Lombards to take a major stake in the company. The first Argonaut, G-ALHS, was flown into Burnaston on 5 October 1961 and a major modification programme to prepare the fleet for service the following summer was undertaken. Before this could take effect, however, tragedy struck the airline. On the night of 6–7 October 1961, Dakota G-AMSW was operating an inclusive-tour service from Gatwick to Perpignan when it struck

Derby Airways Miles Marathon G-AMEW crosses the fence on final approach to Bournemouth airport in July 1959. (Jerry Hughes)

Mount Canigou in the Pyrenees. All 34 passengers and three crew were lost in this, the carrier's first fatal accident. The Argonaut modification programme was to prove extensive, and two examples were cannibalised for spare parts to support the operation of the other three aircraft. Beginning with G-ALHG, these were reworked to cure a tail-heaviness problem. The rear lounge area that had been installed when they had been delivered to their original operator, the state airline BOAC, was removed and the toilets were relocated to that area. Two more windows were cut into the fuselage, permitting the installation of an extra row of seats and increasing the passenger capacity to 75. As this work was being carried out, G-ALHG became the first aircraft to be repainted with the new Derby Airways livery of dark and light blue with a large 'DA' on the tail fin. The three Argonauts entered service during the winter of 1961–62 on holiday routes out of Bristol and Cardiff and from the Midlands, mainly using Birmingham as the short grass runway at Burnaston was judged to be too short for this heavy aircraft. The Argonauts were only to be seen there when heavy engineering work was necessary. The airline's commercial manager was later to declare that the decision to acquire the Argonauts was a big mistake. Although their initial purchase price was less than the cost of DC-6Bs, they proved expensive to operate, had high seat-mile costs and did not possess the range, passenger capacity or

Miles Marathon G-AMEW awaits another load of passengers at Bournemouth in July 1959. (Jerry Hughes)

cargo doors of the Douglas type. Problems with the Argonauts' Rolls-Royce Merlin piston engines caused delays that led to one major tour operator, Hourmont Travel of Cardiff, transferring all of its inclusive-tour contracts to Cambrian Airways. Despite the problems, the Argonauts soldiered on, and, on 27 February 1962, G-ALHS was used to open a new Birmingham–Jersey scheduled service. A few weeks later, Dakota G-AOGZ inaugurated another new route to Jersey, departing Carlisle on 14 March. On 7 May 1962, it was announced that Burnaston had finally been granted full customs facilities, and that these facilities would be transferred across to the new East Midlands Airport when it opened. The airfield at Carlisle gained a prestigious direct link with London on 28 March 1963, when Derby Airways inaugurated Gatwick–Carlisle–Belfast services. The inaugural flight carried a full load of dignitaries, but morning and evening rotations were only scheduled on Mondays and Wednesdays, and no fare-paying passengers were booked for the first week of operations. The second week fared a little better, with a total of 20 passengers, but things did not improve after that, and the service was dropped on 8 May. During 1963 and 1964, the activities of the Argonauts added some interest to the routine of operations. During July 1963, G-ALHY was ferried from Valencia to Burnaston on three engines for repairs. On landing, the crew managed to bring it to a halt with only some 150ft (50m) of runway remaining before the boundary fence. In August 1964, G-ALHS was hired for the filming of scenes for a new cinema movie, *The High Bright Sun*. For the film, old-style BOAC livery was applied using stickers and the aircraft was filmed carrying out numerous take-offs and landings at RAF Northolt.

On 30 July 1964, the board of Derby Airways announced that, with effect from 1 October that year, the operating name of the airline would change to British Midland Airways, to better reflect the company's coverage of the whole Midlands area. This duly took effect, and British Midland was soon expanding under its new identity, in December 1964 taking over the assets of the failing UK independent carrier Mercury Airlines, including its routes from Liverpool and Leeds Bradford airports to Exeter and to Sandown on the Isle of Wight. Mercury's Birmingham–Manchester–Teesside–Newcastle route was also taken over but was soon dropped. Along with Mercury's routes came much needed office and check-in space at Manchester, and the services of one Michael Bishop, later to rise to the very top of British Midland. At the Farnborough Airshow in September 1964, Derby Airways had

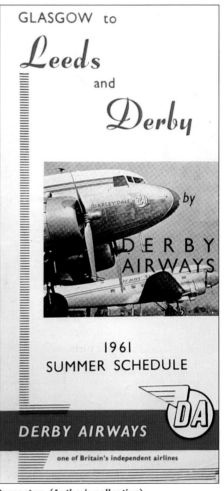

Above left: A 1961 advertisement for Derby Airways services from Burnaston. (Author's collection)

Above right: The cover of the summer 1961 Derby Airways timetable of services from Glasgow to Leeds Bradford and Burnaston, with Dakota illustration. (Author's collection)

Derby Airways Dakota G-AOGZ taxies past two BEA Viscounts parked outside the old terminal building and control tower at Birmingham Airport in July 1962. (H J Black)

signed a £600,000 contract for two pre-used Handley Page Herald srs 200 turbo-prop aircraft. The first of these was handed over in a ceremony at the manufacturer's airfield at Radlett on 1 February 1965 and was delivered to British Midland at Burnaston the same day. For a while, it looked as though British Midland would be acquiring another type of turbo-prop aircraft. On 11 February 1965, the airline issued a statement to the effect that it was considering the purchase of one of the large, four-engined Bristol Britannia srs 102 turbo-prop aircraft that BOAC had for sale. However, nothing was to come of this plan. British Midland was always open to offers of ad hoc charter work, and on 15 March 1965, Dakota G-AMSX, in cargo configuration and with Captain Rothwell in command, carried out a rare sortie behind the 'iron curtain'. The aircraft was flown from Burnaston via Copenhagen to Helsinki, carrying a two-ton power station generator and its associated instrumentation on the first legs of a journey to Moscow. At Helsinki, a Russian navigator and radio operator joined the crew for the onward leg on the following day and were dropped off at Copenhagen on the way back, the whole trip taking a total of 23hrs 20mins flying time.

Chapter 3
A New Home

On 1 April 1965, British Midland's long-awaited transfer to its new operating base at East Midlands Airport was officially completed. Arrangements had been made for the inaugural service into East Midlands on that day to be the return leg of a service setting off from Burnaston for Leeds Bradford and Glasgow and operated by the Herald turbo-prop, G-ASKK. The outbound leg, carrying among its passengers the Lord Mayor of Derby, went off as planned. The Herald had landed at Leeds Bradford on the return journey when fate took a hand. A Dove aircraft of the Civil Aviation Flying Unit was carrying out some approaches to the runway at East Midlands in order to certify the approach lighting when a bulldozer, being used to fill in some ditches close by, became stuck in some mud. During efforts to extricate it, some power lines were severed, blacking out the runway lighting. Dusk was falling and it proved impossible to restore power before dark. A signal was sent to Leeds Bradford instructing the Herald captain to complete the service by flying into Burnaston instead. The aircraft was ferried across to East Midlands on 2 April, and scheduled services commenced on that date instead. In September 1965, British Midland signed an order for two BAC One-Eleven srs 300 jet airliners, intended for use on scheduled services and inclusive-tour flights to leisure destinations. These would have been the company's first completely new aircraft (the Heralds having been leased out to other carriers before delivery to British Midland), but a change of policy resulted in the order being cancelled by the end of March 1966. However, on 21 November 1966, it was announced that negotiations were taking place regarding another One-Eleven order, this time for

Canadair Argonaut G-ALHG in the second version of its Derby Airways livery. This aircraft was lost in a crash at Stockport in 1967 whilst in British Midland service. (Author's collection)

Canadair Argonaut G-ALHN was acquired for spares reclamation only, and is seen here being slowly stripped at Burnaston in July 1964. (Author's collection)

the 'stretched' srs 500 version. These talks led to an eventual order for two examples, later increased to three. In the meantime, Dakota G-AGJV was converted into a freighter and commenced cargo services to the Channel Islands in December 1965, carrying mainly fresh flowers and produce to the mainland on the return legs. The aircraft was to continue in this role until it was finally disposed of in 1969. On 10 January 1967, British Midland began its long and successful association with the four-engined Vickers Viscount turbo-prop aircraft. On that date, srs 736 G-AODG was handed over to the airline at Jersey airport. A second example, srs 831 G-ASED, was delivered to East Midlands Airport on 15 February of that year, releasing Herald G-ASKK, which was taken in part-payment for the Viscounts. These two aircraft were initially placed onto the routes to Glasgow and Belfast, doubling the flight frequency and passenger capacity. Over the coming 11 years, British Midland would acquire another 27 examples of the type, although not all of these were in service at any one time. The airport on the Isle of Wight could still only accept Dakota-size aircraft, and as these were soon to be disposed of with the exception of the freighter G-AGJV, it was decided to terminate the passenger services to the island. At around this time, British Midland intimated that it was hoping to add some former BEA Vickers Vanguard aircraft to its fleet, but none of these large turbo-prop machines were eventually acquired. By June 1967, several Viscounts were in service, and the Argonauts were nearing retirement. They were still used for inclusive-tour flights, and on 4 June 1967, G-ALHG was approaching Manchester at the end of a service from Majorca when two of its engines cut out due to fuel flow problems. It became apparent that the aircraft was not going to reach the runway at Manchester and its commander took the decision to put it down on a patch of waste ground among a built-up area of Stockport. Sixty-nine passengers and three crew members lost their lives in the crash-landing, but

Argonaut G-ALHS in British Midland livery taxies in at Luton in July 1967. (Author)

Argonaut G-ALHY in Derby Airways livery at Newcastle. (Author's collection)

there were no additional casualties on the ground. The two remaining Argonauts were withdrawn from service at the end of the 1967 holiday season and later scrapped.

In 1968, Lombard Banking disposed of its shareholding in British Midland, enabling Minster Assets to step in and take a large stake in the airline, injecting substantially more capital. By the end of that year, the fleet stood at seven Viscounts plus the freighter Dakota. The Viscounts were all srs 700s but had been acquired from a variety of sources and were of a miscellany of sub-types, a fact that was to cause the airline headaches with crew rostering and spares sourcing for some years to come. By February 1969, Minster Assets controlled British Midland and another UK independent carrier, Manston-based Invicta Airways, and announced plans to merge the two airlines. Invicta's two Viscount srs 700s were to join British Midland's passenger fleet, while its small fleet of Douglas C-54A freighters was to operate under the name of British Midland-Invicta Cargo. The merger was duly carried through but was only to last a few weeks. On 7 July 1969, the Invicta board members announced that they were setting up on their own again with a new freight carrier named Invicta Air Cargo. The C-54As went with them, but British Midland retained the two Viscounts. With two Viscounts being lost during the early months of that year, 1969 had got off to a bad start. On 20 February, the first example to be acquired, G-AODG, was written off, fortunately without casualties, in a landing accident during a snowstorm at East Midlands. Then, on 20 March, tragedy struck. G-AVJA was being positioned without passengers from Manchester to Edinburgh when it crashed on take-off and all the crew, apart from one stewardess, were killed. In November 1969, British Midland opened services between Teesside and Heathrow, a route that had previously been operated by Autair and, before that, by BKS Air Transport. The route gave the airline access to London's major aerial gateway, but was to prove hard to operate profitably, initially being flown by Viscount aircraft on a twice-each-weekday basis with an en route stop at East Midlands. During 1969, Michael Bishop began his rise to the top of the airline, being appointed general manager. In March 1970, he was to become a director.

Two generations of airliner. Argonaut G-ALHY, with a British Midland Herald turbo-prop aircraft in the background. (Author's collection)

Derby Airways Dakota G-AGJV. This aircraft was later converted to a freighter for service with British Midland. (Tony Clarke collection via D Whitworth)

Derby Airways Argonaut G-ALHG in a striking climbing pose. (Tony Clarke collection via D Whitworth)

Viscount srs 736 G-AODG was the first Viscount to be acquired by British Midland. (Tony Clarke collection via D Whitworth)

Viscount srs 755 G-AOCB was acquired by British Midland as a result of the ill-fated merger with Invicta Airways in 1969. (Tony Clarke collection via D Whitworth)

Derby Airways Argonaut G-ALHS landing at Berlin (Tempelhof) in April 1963. (Ralf Manteufel)

Derby Airways Argonaut G-ALHS landing at Berlin (Tempelhof) in December 1963. (Ralf Manteufel)

Above: Argonaut G-ALHY in British Midland livery at Southampton. (Barry Friend collection)

Right: Dakota G-APBC in British Midland livery at Southampton in 1967. In the background is a Bristol 170 Superfreighter of British United Airways. (Barry Friend)

Below: Viscount 755 G-AOCB, seen here at Southampton in 1969, was acquired as a result of the short-lived merger with Invicta Airways. (Barry Friend)

Chapter 4
Into the Jet Age

In January 1970, British Midland took delivery of the first of the three BAC One-Eleven srs 523 jets on order. These were 119-seaters, primarily intended for use on the inclusive-tour flight network, and, in order to simplify and speed up the cabin service, pre-packaged cold catering was clipped into a recess in each seatback just before departure. In a bid to upgrade the Teesside–Heathrow service, the One-Eleven aircraft were also placed onto this service, which then became non-stop, with a third rotation each day being introduced from 4 May 1970. The service was certainly improved, but the larger aircraft meant a lot more seats to fill. As a promotion, the airline mailed out vouchers for free flights to 1,500 regular business travellers in the Teesside area during a five-month trial period. Uptake of the vouchers exceeded 800, and gave the airline the confidence to place the service onto a permanent basis at the end of the trial. By 1970, British Midland had 11 Viscounts of varying models in service. On 22 January, the passengers and crew on one of them, srs 814 G-AWXI, had a narrow escape. The aircraft had barely lifted off from Heathrow on a service to Teesside when its number four engine caught fire and the flames spread quickly to the starboard wing. The crew skilfully brought the Viscount back for an emergency landing and only minor injuries were sustained by the 38 passengers during the evacuation. However, investigators later estimated that the wing would have failed after another 20 seconds or so of flight.

Former British United Airways Viscount srs 831 G-APNE at East Midlands Airport. (Author)

The fulfilment of the One-Eleven order allowed the airline to dispose of its early 700 srs Viscounts and standardise on the later srs 810 version. The One-Elevens were introduced from May 1970 onto inclusive-tour flights and some scheduled services out of East Midlands. The holiday charters out of East Midlands were not to prove a great success, as very few tour operators were willing to offer departures from this comparatively obscure airport, and British Midland was forced to lay on expensive positioning flights prior to services out of airports such as Manchester, Birmingham and Luton. Charter rates remained low in 1970, and the jet fleet of just three One-Elevens was insufficient to cover the tour programme as well as the scheduled services. At the end of March 1971, the Viscounts returned to the Teesside–Heathrow route, although this time on a non-stop basis. In order to free up Viscount availability for this change, however, the airline's Leeds Bradford to Glasgow route had to be suspended. In 1972, British Midland took the decision to withdraw from the inclusive-tour market and dispose of its One-Elevens. One was leased to Court Line Aviation and another was sold, but the remaining example was retained for a limited series of holiday charters out of Bristol, East Midlands and Luton until 1974. During the financial year ending 30 September 1971, the airline recorded a loss of £1,671,733. It was decided to adopt a policy of expanding the scheduled service network and acquiring still more Viscounts.

Throughout this uncertain period, the airline's backer, Minster Assets, had not lost faith in it, investing a further £1.5 million in early 1970. That year, British Midland entered a new and radically different sphere of activity, the transatlantic passenger charter market. In March 1970, the airline applied to the US Civil Aeronautics Board for a Foreign Carrier Permit to operate group charter flights between Europe and the US. Whilst the application was pending, British Midland looked around for suitable long-haul jet equipment for the routes and acquired a former Pan

Former South African Airways Viscount srs 813 G-AZLP at Liverpool. (Author)

Former Qantas Boeing 707-338C G-BFLE in between leases at East Midlands Airport in September 1981. (Author)

American Airways Boeing 707-321. Placed on the UK register as G-AYBJ, this aircraft was handed over to the airline at Nassau, in the Bahamas, on 1 April 1970. Following a period of intensive crew training at Miami, the 189-seat 707 was ferried across the Atlantic via Gander and Keflavik, arriving at East Midlands on 26 April and becoming the largest aircraft to have landed there at that time. The Foreign Carrier Permit application was duly approved by US President Nixon and issued on 2 June. The aircraft began earning its keep later that month when it carried members of an international friendship club between Stansted and New York. Most of this aircraft's early work originated from this Essex airport, carrying groups of passengers to Toronto and the Caribbean as well as New York. A second ex-Pan American example, registered G-AYVE, was placed into service during March 1971, and, in August of that year, British Midland operated its first transatlantic charter flight out of Teesside airport. Some flights to the US used East Midlands airport, but following passenger complaints about the lack of permanent immigration and foreign exchange facilities there, the airline issued a statement saying there would be no expansion of its transatlantic services from the airport until these problems were addressed. In addition to Europe-originating charter work, British Midland was also able to secure contracts for transatlantic flights originating in the US, operating a series of charters from Seattle to East Midlands via Keflavik during the summer of 1971. There was still some Boeing 707 capacity available for one-off flights, and, on 21 May 1971, one of these aircraft carried 130 passengers on a Manchester–Ostend scheduled service. From 1972, British Midland, along with other UK airlines operating transatlantic group

236D2 179 923

Domestic Routes
Passenger Ticket and Baggage Check

BMA

British Midland

The friendly independent

Issued by British Midland East Midlands Airport Derby UK

Cover of ticket issued to author by British Midland, 'The Friendly Independent', for travel Liverpool–Heathrow and return in March 1981. (Author's collection)

charter flights, encountered complaints from the licencing authorities, alleging infringements of the 'affinity-group' membership regulations. Early that year, the US Civil Aeronautics Board (CAB) named BOAC, Air India and British Midland in a lawsuit accusing these companies of carrying charter passengers who were not members of a bona fide eligible group. The CAB and the UK Civil Aviation Authority introduced spot checks on passengers boarding on both sides of the Atlantic, resulting in departure delays and even in some flights being cancelled at the last moment. In June 1972, the CAB announced that, because of continuing violations of the rules, the UK independent carriers British Midland, Dan-Air, and Lloyd International Airways would, from 1 July 1972, have to obtain prior approval from them for each individual charter flight to the US. By that time, the scheduled service carriers, such as BOAC, Pan American and TWA, had reacted to the charter flight threat by introducing cheap, advance-purchase fares on their scheduled services. These fares were available to anyone without membership of a group, legitimate or otherwise. They had also introduced wide-bodied Boeing 747 jets onto their services, and the charter 707s were losing their passenger appeal. British Midland took the decision to withdraw almost completely from the North Atlantic charter market and switch the 707s onto long-haul inclusive-tour flights to the Caribbean, the Far East and Africa.

Meanwhile back in 1971, Michael Bishop had been allocated a budget of £135,000 with which to acquire more Viscounts. During a long-haul flight, he was perusing the 'aircraft for sale' columns of an aviation magazine when he saw that South African Airways (SAA) were putting their fleet of Viscount srs 813s on the market. As soon as could be arranged, he made a trip to Johannesburg and offered to buy two of the aircraft, only to be told that SAA were only considering offers for the entire fleet of seven aircraft plus spare parts. With nothing to lose, he submitted a bid of £98,000 for the fleet, plus a further £37,000 for the spares package, and was pleasantly surprised when his offer was accepted. As the aircraft arrived in the UK, they underwent a major refurbishment programme, which included the reduction of their seating capacity from 78 to 73. The arrival of the extra Viscounts was timely, as, on 1 February 1972, the Southend-based independent airline Channel Airways had ceased operations. For the sum of £100,000, British Midland acquired some of that airline's route licences, adding services out of Southend, Bournemouth and Stansted to

Jersey and Guernsey to its portfolio. The company also successfully bid at auction for a package of former Channel Airways Viscount training aids, enabling it to henceforth run its own Rolls-Royce Dart engine training courses. By June 1972, all seven of the former SAA Viscounts were in service, and British Midland could standardise on the later srs 810 aircraft and dispose of its older assorted models. On 10 April 1972, former SAA Viscount G-AZLT inaugurated new British Midland services linking East Midlands and Birmingham with Frankfurt and Brussels. Evidence that the airline was now on a sound financial footing came in September 1972, with the announcement that its issued share capital had been increased to just over £5m in order to provide for further development, in particular the continued expansion of the scheduled services network. The airline's profile in this respect was raised on 1 November 1972, with the opening of British Midland's first check-in desk in Heathrow's new Terminal One. Prior to this date, the company had been reliant on BEA for these services.

Late November 1972 saw the development of British Midland's 'instant-airline' concept – the hiring out of Boeing 707 aircraft, with flight crews and with or without cabin crews and technical assistance, to airlines in developing African or Asian countries. One of the early customers was Sudan Airways, a Comet 4C operator that was looking to become a 'big jet' airline and expand its route network. It was seeking a reputable established airline to operate long-haul services on its behalf until it was ready to take these over with its own aircraft and personnel. A deal was struck whereby British Midland would lease Boeing 707s, complete with flight crews, to Sudan Airways for operation on that carrier's 'Blue Nile' jet service to Europe. The £3.3m contract included the training of flight deck and cabin crew at East Midlands Airport and initially covered the period to the end of 1973. It would almost fully utilise both of British Midland's 707s, although there would still be some weekend availability for ad hoc charter work. The aircraft interiors were reconfigured with 211 seats and additional

British Aerospace One-Eleven srs 523 G-AXLM was originally acquired for inclusive-tour flights. (David Whitworth)

Boeing 707-338C G-BFLE was originally built for service with Qantas. (Rob Hodgkins)

Former South African Airways Viscount srs 813 G-AZNA. (Trevor Hall)

emergency exits, and, on 11 November 1972, G-AYBJ operated between Heathrow and Khartoum at the commencement of the Sudan Airways lease. This proved so successful that the contract was later extended until mid-summer 1974. When it eventually came to an end, Boeing 707 G-AYVE was refurbished, refitted with just 189 seats, repainted in British Midland livery, and went on contract to British Caledonian Airways for three months from July 1974, operating out of Gatwick, Manchester and Prestwick to Canada, the US and Africa. More work was found for the 707s when British Midland leased both aircraft to the Israeli airline El Al, and, on 10 August 1974, G-AYBJ was despatched from East Midlands to Baghdad at the start of a three-month lease to Iraqi Airways. One ad hoc 707 charter made the headlines in April 1975 when G-AYVE was hired by the Daily Mail newspaper to fly out to Saigon during the final days of the Vietnam War and bring 150 orphaned Vietnamese children back to the UK. There was obviously work for more than two Boeing 707s, and, by the end of 1975, British Midland had expanded its fleet to six examples. These were kept gainfully employed over the next five years on passenger-carrying work on behalf of various airlines, including the East African Airways Corporation, Nigeria Airways, Kuwait Airways, Yemen Airways, Air Algerie, Syrian Arab Airways, LAM of Mozambique and Ariana Afghan Airlines, and on cargo services for Pakistan International Airways and Malaysian Airlines System. During the Kuwait Airways contract, Boeing 707 G-AWZA was hijacked whilst flying between Beirut and Kuwait. The incident ended on the tarmac at Damascus Airport, fortunately without casualties. Many of these contracts were for periods in excess of a year, and, on 4 February 1977, two leased British Midland 707s flew the inaugural schedules of the newly formed Kenya Airways. Availability could still be found for the occasional unusual charter, including a three-week operation transporting salmon from King Salmon Airport in Alaska to Abbotsford, near Vancouver. Not all of the 'instant airline' operations utilised Boeing 707s. On 5 February 1975, Viscount srs 813s G-AZLR and G-AZLT departed East Midlands for Cyprus to open new air services out of Larnaca on lease to Cyprus Airways.

Viscount srs 813 G-AZLS at the Coventry airport. (Rob Hodgkins)

Former South African Airways (SAA) Viscount srs 813 G-AZLS at the East Midlands Airport base. (Mick Bajcar)

Meanwhile, back in the UK, 1972 saw mixed developments for British Midland. Michael Bishop continued his rapid progress to the top, being appointed the airline's managing director, but the company recorded a loss of £846,000 for the financial year. Much of this was attributed to a shortfall in revenue from the transatlantic charter operations. Further development at Heathrow came on 30 April 1973, with the inauguration of services from Newquay in Cornwall, initially using Viscount equipment. The same aircraft then continued onward on another inaugural service, this time from Heathrow to Strasbourg. The significance of the granting of a licence for this latter route, British Midland's first international route out of Heathrow, would become apparent in later years. Fleet re-equipment continued with the disposal of two of the One-Elevens to the Brazilian operator Trans Brasil. As part of the deal, British Midland acquired three of that company's Herald aircraft, with the first example arriving at East Midlands on 23 March 1973, after a marathon delivery flight from South America. Four Viscount srs 814s, which had originally been delivered to Lufthansa, were also purchased, bringing the airline's Viscount total to 12 basically similar airframes. From October 1973, the ongoing conflict in the Middle East between Israel and its neighbours, Egypt and Syria, led to the Organisation of Arab Petroleum Exporting Countries restricting supplies of oil to countries supporting Israel. The restrictions led to a doubling and re-doubling of the price of aviation fuel. Fuel rationing was imposed, and some scheduled services had to be discontinued. By the time rationing ended in April 1974, air fares had increased by 20 per cent. The search for other, less vulnerable, sources of oil accelerated exploration in the North Sea and, for much of 1974, two of the Heralds were stationed at Aberdeen airport on lucrative oil rig support contracts.

The mid-1970s saw the introduction of another jet type to the British Midland aircraft inventory in the shape of the twin-engined Douglas DC-9. Two used examples of the short-fuselage srs 14 and 15 variants were acquired during 1976 and 1977, with the first one, US-registered srs 15 N65358, arriving at East Midlands from Arizona on 27 August 1976. As British Midland was the first UK

Viscount srs 813 G-AZLR at East Midlands Airport in 1974. (Mick Bajcar)

Boeing 707-321F G-AZWA was wet-leased to Kuwait Airways in 1975 and again in 1976. (Rob Hodgkins)

DC-9 operator, it had to shoulder the financial burden of the extensive modifications required to place the aircraft onto the UK register some 20 months later. For the 1976 summer season, all of British Midland's scheduled services were operated by Viscount 800 series or Handley Page Herald turbo-prop equipment. The Viscounts operated the prestige international routes linking East Midlands and Birmingham with Paris (Le Bourget), Brussels, Frankfurt and Amsterdam, and the business-oriented routes out of East Midlands to Glasgow, Belfast and Dublin, while the Heralds maintained the more leisure-oriented services from East Midlands and Birmingham to the Isle of Man, and seasonal flights to Jersey from Coventry, Birmingham, East Midlands and Luton. A high-frequency link between Heathrow and Birmingham was operated in co-operation with British Airways. British Midland utilised Herald aircraft, while the state airline used larger Viscount srs 800s. The first DC-9 entered service on the Heathrow–Teesside route on 27 September 1976. That year was a financially difficult one for the airline. The 'instant airline' business was beginning to decline as customer airlines introduced their own jet equipment, and three of the 707s were taken out of service. Big cutbacks were announced just before Christmas, and, in the early part of the 1977, the Viscount fleet was trimmed down to just the seven srs 813s. By 1978, British Midland was moving forward once more. The frequencies on the routes linking East Midlands and Birmingham with Brussels and Frankfurt were upgraded, and Michael Bishop was appointed chairman. On 25 January that year, he flew into Liverpool aboard a British Midland Boeing 707 for secret talks with local authorities on the future of that city's air services. These discussions culminated with the announcement on 11 May 1978 of a route-swap arrangement with British Airways. The national carrier was to hand over all of its routes out of Liverpool to British Midland in exchange for routes linking Birmingham with Brussels, Frankfurt and Copenhagen. British Midland was to base three Viscounts and a DC-9

Viscount srs 813 G-AZLS painted up for lease to Cyprus Airways. (Rob Hodgkins)

at Liverpool to operate the former British Airways services to Heathrow, Belfast, the Isle of Man, Glasgow and the Channel Islands. This arrangement was approved by the Civil Aviation Authority on 14 July 1978, to take effect from the end of October that year. On 29 October, the former Finnair DC-9 srs 14 OH-LYB operated British Midland's inaugural Liverpool–Heathrow service. By 1978, British Midland's directors had ambitious plans for expansion but were unsure if sufficient funding would be forthcoming from Minster Assets, and the idea of a management buy-out was discussed. Michael Bishop, General Manager John Wolfe, and Financial Director Stuart Balmforth set up British Midland Holdings as a vehicle for any possible buy-out and began searching for a further partner to complete the funding. They found this in the possibly unlikely form of Robert F Beauchamp, the wealthy Californian owner of a chain of dental practices in the US. He contributed 25 per cent of the capital as his stake and also loaned the other partners the funds to enable British Midland Holdings to acquire a 75 per cent controlling interest in the airline. On 21 July 1978, Minster Assets announced that it was to dispose of British Midland Airways to the above-mentioned partners for the sum of £2.875m. Michael Bishop then took a 51 per cent stake in British Midland Holdings. The business name of the airline was registered as simply 'British Midland', although the trading name remained British Midland Airways. In August 1979, British Airways announced a further restructuring of its UK internal route network. It would be pulling out completely from six UK airports and handing over some unprofitable domestic routes to independent carriers. As a result of this policy, British Midland gained licences for services linking Heathrow with Leeds Bradford and the Isle of Man, and from Birmingham and Glasgow to the Channel Islands. During 1979, British Midland Airways carried one-million passengers in a year for the first time in its history. By 1980, British Midland was in need of proper, permanent premises for its administrative departments, which were still housed in prefabricated buildings scattered around the perimeter of East Midlands Airport. During that spring, the airline discovered Donington Hall, a disused stately home lying just outside the airport boundary. The necessary finance to support the purchase for £185,000 was secured, and, over the next 18 months, a programme of total restoration and refurbishment transformed the mansion into a fully integrated and computerised headquarters building, into which British Midland were to relocate in September 1982.

Handley Page Herald G-BAVX was acquired from Sadia in Brazil. (Trevor Hall)

Former Sadia Herald G-ATIG at East Midlands Airport. (Mick Bajcar)

This short-fuselage DC-9 is still carrying its former Finnair registration letters, OH-LYD, at Edinburgh. (Graham Marchbank)

Above: DC-9-15 G-BMAA in the original British Midland livery. This DC-9 later became the first British Midland aircraft to wear the 'Diamond' colour scheme. (Rob Hodgkins)

Left: Former Finnair DC-9-14 G-BMAH. (Trevor Hall)

Below: The last Viscount in British Midland service was the former SAA srs 813 G-AZNA, seen here at East Midlands in March 1985. (Kev Colbran)

Your Local Travel Agent

BMA BRITISH MIDLAND AIRWAYS

BMA BRITISH MIDLAND AIRWAYS
Winter timetable & fares
November '69 – March '70

Right and below: DC-9-14 G-BMAH landing at Heathrow in July 1986. (Kev Colbran)

Derby Airways' first Dakota G-ANTD survived as a freighter and was repainted in British Midland livery. It is seen here at Berlin (Tempelhof) in September 1966, with the nose of a Saturn Airways DC-7C behind it. (Ralf Manteufel)

Boeing 707-338C G-BFLE in an interim livery between leases at Berlin (Tempelhof) in June 1981. (Ralf Manteufel)

Both sides of a medallion issued by British Midland Airways in 1978 to commemorate 40 years of operations. One side has silhouettes of Dakota, Marathon, Argonaut, Viscount and DC-9 aircraft. (Author's collection)

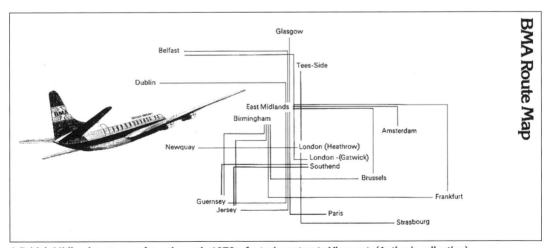

A British Midland route map from the early 1970s, featuring a trusty Viscount. (Author's collection)

British Midland Airways
Winter Timetable & Fares

VALID NOVEMBER 1st 1974–
MARCH 31st 1975

BMA

G-AY

2nd Edition

The cover of the winter 1974–75 British Midland timetable, featuring
the tail of a Boeing 707, not to be found operating any of the
scheduled services contained therein. (Author's collection)

Chapter 5

Competing with British Airways

In June 1982, British Midland and the British and Commonwealth Group, the owners of the UK independent airline Air UK, announced that they were jointly going to revive Manx Airlines, a dormant Isle of Man-based airline, and transfer to it all of their routes serving that island. Ownership was to be split 75/25 in favour of British Midland, which would contribute its prime Heathrow–Isle of Man route and one Viscount aircraft. Air UK would add two Fokker F-27 turbo-props and a leased Bandeirante feeder-liner aircraft to complete the initial fleet. Manx Airlines was to suffer losses of over £300,000 in its first financial year, largely attributed to the high operating costs of its elderly fleet, and its parent company soon invested in more modern aircraft for it, beginning with two Shorts 360s, which were delivered in March 1984. The establishment of Manx Airlines was the beginning of the British Midland group of companies, in which Manx Airlines was soon to be joined by Loganair. This Glasgow-based airline had operated mainly within Scotland until 1982, when it was awarded routes linking Manchester with Glasgow, Edinburgh and Belfast. By then, it was experiencing financial difficulties and its owner, the Royal Bank of Scotland, was seeking a buyer. British Midland

DC-9 srs 32 G-BMAK in the 'Diamond' livery at Edinburgh in 1994. (Author)

Loganair Fokker F-27 G-BMAP. (Eric Melrose)

Left: **Fokker F-27 G-BLGW in early British Midland livery. (Lewis Grant)**

Below: **Fokker F-27 G-BMAS on take-off, wearing its early British Midland livery. (Rob Hodgkins)**

could see that its route system would dovetail neatly with its own and opened negotiations that would lead to Loganair becoming a subsidiary in December 1983. By then, British Midland had accomplished a major feat in securing the rights to compete directly with the British Airways no-prebooking 'Shuttle' service on the trunk routes from Heathrow to Glasgow, Edinburgh and Belfast. Services to Glasgow were inaugurated on 25 October 1982, with British Midland's seven daily round-trips filling time slots between the British Airways flights and offering lower fares and a meal service. Full-service flights to Edinburgh and Belfast followed in March 1983 and March 1984, respectively, and their success in attracting passengers forced British Airways to upgrade its own flights to 'Super Shuttle' standard, complete with meal service and a complimentary bar, from September 1983.

At the beginning of the 1980s, Britain experienced another financial recession. Air travel declined and British Midland was forced to reduce its passenger capacity to match the diminished demand. Viscounts were re-introduced in place of DC-9s on many routes and two of the jets were put into storage during the winter of 1980–81. Smaller, but more modern, turbo-prop aircraft were acquired,

Right: British Midland initially used leased Shorts 330 G-BJFK on East Midlands–Heathrow schedules. (Lewis Grant)

Below: Former Finnair DC-9-14 G-BMAH on pushback at Glasgow airport. (Graham Marchbank)

Former KLM DC-9-15 G-BMAG at East Midlands. (Eric Melrose)

DC-9-15 G-BMAB at Birmingham airport. (Eric Melrose)

beginning with a 30-seat Shorts 330 G-BJFK leased from the manufacturer and introduced onto the East Midlands–Heathrow route in October 1981. The success of this type in service led to an order for six examples of the developed Shorts 360, introduced in 1983, also used by Loganair and Manx Airlines and praised by Michael Bishop as 'the best aircraft we've ever operated'. By the summer of 1983, thanks largely to the traffic on the domestic trunk routes, British Midland had grown to become the second-busiest operator at Heathrow after British Airways, when measured in terms of aircraft movements. By mid-1984, the fleet comprised eight DC-9s, seven Fokker F-27s, three Viscounts, three Boeing 707s (mainly used for inclusive-tour flights) and two Shorts 360s. Faced with stringent new noise regulations, British Midland disposed of its last Boeing 707s in 1984. From October 1985 until March 1987, British Midland's own aircraft were to be supplemented by BAC One-Eleven srs 300 G-WLAD, leased from Airways International Cymru, and largely used on the Leeds Bradford–Heathrow route. By 1984, the US was in the midst of a financial recession and Dr Beauchamp was looking to divest himself of his investment in British Midland in order to raise some capital. In July 1984, his three partners in the airline raised the necessary funding and bought out his shareholding. During 1985, British Midland placed an order for three examples of the new 72-seat British Aerospace ATP high-tech turbo-prop aircraft, with options on three more. By the summer of that year, the carrier was serving eight destinations from Heathrow, four from East Midlands, and two from Birmingham. Another momentous day in the development of the airline was 29 June 1986, which was the date it launched its first jet international scheduled service between Heathrow and Amsterdam, in direct competition with British Airways and KLM. DC-9 aircraft were used, British Midland having, by then, built up a fleet of six short-fuselage srs 15s and two examples of the longer srs 32 version. The carrier's struggle to secure traffic rights for the service had benefitted from the fact that it had operated Heathrow–Strasbourg services during the 1970s. Although these were no longer active, they helped

DC-9-32 G-BMAK at Edinburgh. (Eric Melrose)

Shorts 360 G-BMAJ on final approach. (Lewis Grant)

the airline to lay claim to so-called 'grandfather rights' as an established international operator at the airport.

During the summer of 1986, the airline underwent a major image restyling, with the introduction of 'Diamond Service' branding on its flights. This featured hot meals and complimentary drinks in flight and was initially introduced on the domestic trunk routes out of Heathrow, eventually being rolled out across the whole of the route network. A new aircraft livery featuring a dark blue upper fuselage and a red 'BM' enclosing a silver diamond shape on the tailfin was gradually applied to the fleet. On 1 September 1987, the Diamond Club frequent flyer programme, offering members access to dedicated airport lounges, was unveiled. To coincide with the launch of the programme, British Midland introduced a new practice of naming its DC-9s after famous diamonds, with G-PKBM being christened 'The Tiffany Diamond' by the managing director of the Tiffany & Co jewellery house on 1 September. By then, however, British Midland had already decided on a new type of aircraft to replace the ageing DC-9s, placing an order for six (later increased to eight) Boeing 737 srs 300s, configured to carry 136 passengers. The McDonnell Douglas MD-80 development of the DC-9 had also been considered, but had lost out because of its smaller hold space for the carriage of lucrative mail on the domestic trunk routes out of Heathrow and its inability to lift a full payload from the short runway at Jersey. The 737 entered service on 1 December 1987, with a flight from Heathrow to Edinburgh.

In 1986, another subsidiary had been added to the British Midland portfolio. The new London City Airport had been built in the Docklands area of the capital and Eurocity Express was established to operate from there to Paris, Amsterdam, Brussels, Manchester and the Channel Islands using two DHC-7 short take-off and landing turbo-props leased from the manufacturer. The original intention was to operate in partnership with Air France on the Paris route, but this arrangement did

ATP turbo-prop G-BMYM taxiing at Heathrow. (Kerry Taylor)

not come about and Eurocity Express instead co-operated with the Belgian national carrier Sabena on flights to Brussels. This route and the one to Paris (Charles De Gaulle) were inaugurated on 26 October 1987. Towards the end of that year, the airline was renamed London City Airways and became part of Airlines of Britain plc, a new holding company set up to encompass British Midland and its subsidiaries. During the following year, services to Amsterdam were added and the business travel-oriented routes were supplemented by summer services to Jersey and occasional charter flights at weekends. Three new DHC-7s (the last ones to be built) were ordered and, following their delivery, the leased examples were handed back. A fourth, used, example joined London City Airways in 1988, but without the planned partnership with Air France the services were never going to be commercially viable. The London City operations were scaled down, then transferred to the parent company in 1990, but, by the end of 1991, British Midland had withdrawn completely from the airport. British Midland said a fond farewell to the Viscount on 19 February 1988 when srs 813 G-AZNA operated the company's last scheduled service with the type from Brussels to Birmingham. This was not the final goodbye, however, as on the following day this aircraft carried out a special enthusiasts' flight from East Midlands to Bournemouth and return and was later to be leased out to Manx Airlines. On 9 May 1988, the company inaugurated services with its new ATP turbo-prop aircraft, initially rostering the type onto East Midlands–Amsterdam and high frequency Heathrow–Birmingham rotations. The ATP had been acquired to replace the remaining Viscounts and to supplement the DC-9s. It was to prove reliable and economical in operation but suffered from an image problem with its propellor power plants. Passengers perceived it as old-fashioned, and its service with British Midland was short-lived, although it served for longer with subsidiaries Manx and Loganair. During June 1988, the Airlines of Britain group bought out Air UK's minority stake in Manx Airlines. More financial manoeuvring in December

1988 saw the Scandinavian Airlines System (SAS) paying £35m for a 24.9 per cent (increased to 40 per cent in 1994) stake in British Midland. However, 1989 began with a disaster. On 8 January, Boeing 737 srs 400 G-OBME was operating flight BD092 from Heathrow to Belfast with 118 passengers and eight crew members on board. As the flight approached the Midlands, its crew reported vibration in one of the two engines and shut down what was later found to have been the healthy one. The aircraft was diverted for a precautionary landing at East Midlands, but the crew were able to maintain height using the remaining, unhealthy, engine. Whilst on final approach, the aircraft struck the M1 motorway near Kegworth and ended up broken on the embankment. Forty-seven passengers lost their lives.

ATP G-BMYL on final approach to Heathrow in 1988. (Kerry Taylor)

ATP G-MANL at Paris (CDG). (Denis Deparis)

Above: BAC One-Eleven srs 300 G-WLAD was leased from Airways Cymru International and frequently used on Leeds Bradford–Heathrow schedules. (Rob Hodgkins)

Right: DC-9 srs 32 G-ELDI at Edinburgh. (Graham Marchbank)

Below: Viscount srs 813 G-AZNA operated the last British Midland Viscount service and was the only example to wear the 'Diamond' livery. (Kerry Taylor)

Eurocity Express DHC-7 turbo-prop G-BNDC was used on services out of London City Airport. (Lewis Grant)

Boeing 737 srs 400 G-OBMO at Newcastle. (Graham Marchbank)

Boeing 737 srs 400 G-OBMG at Edinburgh in 1989. (Eric Melrose)

Boeing 737 srs 300 G-OBMA at Edinburgh in 1989. (Eric Melrose)

Above: Boeing 737 srs 300 G-OBMB at Glasgow in 1989. (Eric Melrose)

Left: F-27 srs 200 G-BMAW landing at Heathrow in July 1986. (Kev Colbran)

Below: After the termination of the London City services, the DHC-7 aircraft were transferred to the parent company. G-BOAY is seen at Heathrow in March 1988. (Kev Colbran)

Above: DC-9-32 G-PKBM on finals to Heathrow in September 1988. (Barry Friend collection)

Right: A September 1983 advertisement for British Midland's UK domestic network, including a 'dig' at the competition. (Author's collection)

The friendly way to the regions from Heathrow.

Who's the second busiest airline at Heathrow these days?

Surprise! It's British Midland, with 36 departures every working day.

We got there by putting the customer first, with friendly, full service flights to the North, the Midlands—and now Scotland.

It seems our flights to Glasgow and Edinburgh are so good that even a certain other airline has decided its got to try harder too!

British Midland
The friendly independent
RESERVATIONS: 01-581 0864

Chapter 6

Restructuring and Revamps

I n 1991, the Airlines of Britain group was restructured. Manx Airlines continued to serve its core routes out of the Isle of Man, but all its other domestic and European services were transferred to a new Manx Airlines Europe company, based at Cardiff airport. During the early 1990s, British Midland pursued a policy of adding a small number of European destinations to its route network each year. In 1992, Heathrow–Brussels, Glasgow–Frankfurt and East Midlands–Frankfurt were added to the portfolio. By then, the airline was operating a mixed fleet comprising 15 Boeing 737s and 13 DC-9s. Not all of the company's routes stood the test of time. In October 1993, the East Midlands–Heathrow service was suspended, and the East Midlands–Belfast route was transferred to Manx Airlines Europe. During 1993–96, the fleet was upgraded with the addition of eight Boeing 737 srs 500s and the acquisition of new Dutch-built twin-jets in the shape of three Fokker 70s and four Fokker 100s. During 1994, the majority of Loganair's fleet and its network of business-oriented routes around the UK were transferred to Manx Airlines Europe, leaving Loganair with just the Scottish 'highlands and islands' routes and its Islander aircraft. In 1995, Manx Airlines Europe became a British Airways franchise carrier, operating as British Airways Express. It was to be renamed again in September 1996, becoming British Regional Air Lines. On 29 April 1996, services between East Midlands and Aberdeen

Boeing 737 srs 500 G-OBMZ in a later version of the British Midland livery at East Midlands Airport. (Eric Melrose)

Above: Boeing 737 srs 300 G-ODSK, seen here at Edinburgh in April 1998 in the bmi 'Diamond' livery, was later transferred to the fleet of low-cost subsidiary bmibaby. (Eric Melrose)

Right: Boeing 737 srs 300 G-ODSK in the bmi British Midland Airways livery. (Eric Melrose)

Boeing 737 srs 500 G-BVZG in the bmi British Midland Airways livery. (Eric Melrose)

were launched, bringing the number of destinations served from the Midlands airport to 13. Two other notable events that month were the departure of the last British Midland DC-9 from East Midlands on 10 April, and the signing of a co-operation agreement with Lufthansa, which led to code-sharing in timetables and on airport departure boards. On 30 September 1996, British Midland unveiled its latest series of product improvements. These included new Jaeger-inspired cabin crew uniforms, lounge access at all UK airports served, new seats in Euroclass cabins and the extension of this class onto all domestic services. With the introduction of this measure, British Midland became the first airline to provide separate business class cabins on domestic trunk routes out of Heathrow.

On 27 February 1997, the Airlines of Britain group underwent a further restructuring. The Aberdeen-based Saab 340 operator Business Air (which had been acquired by Manx Airlines in 1996), Loganair and Manx Airlines were hived off as British Regional Airlines (Holdings) Ltd. British Regional Air Lines remained in the hands of senior members of the British Midland management, but all operational links with British Midland were severed in order to avoid possible conflict with its British Airways franchise operations. In 1998, Business Air was renamed British Midland Commuter, soon to be changed again to British Midland Regional. On 14 July 1997, British Midland signed a contract with Airbus Industrie for 11 A320 and nine A321 twin-jet aircraft for delivery from the spring of 1998. Built into the contract was an option to transfer some of the A320s on order to the larger A321 model. The first to be delivered was the 196-seat A321 srs 200 G-MIDA, which was handed over at Belfast on 3 April 1998. The first 150-seat A320 srs 200, G-MIDZ, followed in January 1999. During 1998, more new routes were introduced, including Heathrow–Manchester, Heathrow–Warsaw, Leeds Bradford–Jersey, and holiday services from East Midlands to Palma, Malaga and Faro. An order had also been placed with the Brazilian manufacturer Embraer in 1997 for a fleet of ten 50-seat Embraer 145 jets to serve the shorter routes from the summer of 1999. During 1998, British Midland had, after a 15-year lapse, re-entered the transatlantic route tussle with an application for licences to serve

Bmi Boeing 737 srs 500 G-BVZH at Heathrow. (Eric Melrose)

Fokker 70 G-BVTE at Paris (Charles de Gaulle) in 1998. (Denis Deparis)

Fokker 70 G-BVTF in the British Midland 'Diamond' livery at Aberdeen in 1997. (Eric Melrose)

ten US cities from Heathrow. This process was to prove lengthy and frustrating. Under the existing UK–US bilateral agreement, only two UK carriers were permitted to operate North Atlantic scheduled services, and British Airways and Virgin Atlantic were already incumbent licence-holders. While awaiting a solution to this stumbling-block, British Midland continued to expand its European activities. During 1999, new routes linking Heathrow with Hanover, Stuttgart and Budapest, and East Midlands with

Frankfurt were inaugurated, but these were to be short-lived. In November 1999, it was announced that Lufthansa had completed negotiations to acquire a 20 per cent stake in British Midland for £91m. This arrangement was conditional upon Lufthansa securing entry for British Midland into the Star Alliance airline grouping. If this could be achieved, then SAS, one of the other members of the Star Alliance, would reduce its shareholding in British Midland to 20 per cent, thus allowing Lufthansa to acquire those shares. The complex negotiations were successfully concluded, and the date of 1 July 2000 was set for British Midland to become the 13th member of the Star Alliance. The airline then entered into a three-way profit-sharing arrangement with Lufthansa and SAS, which included flight number code-sharing on all of the three airlines' flights out of Heathrow and Manchester. In order to eliminate competition with its new partners, British Midland dropped its services to Eastern Europe, launching new routes to Spain and Italy in their place. Some shorter routes, including London–Paris, were also dropped, freeing up slots at Heathrow for hoped-for long-haul services. In anticipation of its entry into the Star Alliance, one of British Midland's aircraft was painted up in Star Alliance livery, being unveiled in the new markings in March 2000.

In 2001, British Airways acquired Manx Airlines and British Regional Air Lines, absorbing them into its own Brymon Airways subsidiary. That year had started with another revamp for British Midland. This name was, by then, considered too parochial for a carrier with global ambitions and a new name was needed. One suggestion considered was British Blue, but this was considered to be too similar to that of the US carrier Jet Blue and the eventual choice was bmi, all in lowercase lettering. In answer to queries on the subject, it was explained that bmi was not an abbreviation for anything, but some confusion still abounded. For two years, the suffix 'British Midland' was appended to the bmi titles while passengers and the public grew used to the new identity, then gradually dropped. A new aircraft livery of two shades of blue, with a 'wave' motif in 'sailing blue' across the fuselage was gradually

Fokker 100 G-BXWE at Paris (Charles de Gaulle) in 1998. (Denis Deparis)

Fokker 100 G-BVJA lifts off from Edinburgh. (Gerry Hill)

applied to the fleet, with the official unveiling taking place at the Heathrow engineering base on 1 February 2001. The British Midland Regional subsidiary, which had been operating many of British Midland's shorter routes with its Embraer jets, was duly rebranded as bmi Regional. The other big development that year was the return of the parent company to the North Atlantic market. Frustrated by the repeated denial of transatlantic rights out of Heathrow, Michael Bishop had successfully applied for licences to serve Washington DC and Chicago from Manchester. As a sign of his commitment to the North Atlantic route, he had ordered three wide-bodied Airbus A330 srs 200 jets for these routes and, hopefully, for use on eventual transatlantic services out of Heathrow. The first example, registered G-WWBM, was delivered in the new bmi livery to Manchester on 27 April 2001 and inaugurated services to Washington on 12 May that year. The second aircraft duly arrived at Manchester on 9 May and opened the Chicago route on 8 June. The third aircraft was accepted on 30 May but, as the Heathrow route applications had still not been granted, went on wet-lease to South African Airways before delivery. The two A330s in bmi service were in a three-cabin configuration, with passengers in the the Business section having their meals freshly prepared and served by an on-board chef. Passengers arriving at Manchester airport were offered a complimentary package of facilities at the Radisson SAS Hotel there, including use of showers, gym and swimming pool. The future looked bright for the new bmi brand, but world events were to intervene. On 11 September 2001, the hijacking of several airliners in the US, and the deliberate crashing of them into the Twin Towers skyscrapers in New York and other targets, brought immediate consequences for airlines everywhere. Air travel worldwide, and especially on the prime North Atlantic routes, went into recession and bmi was forced to put its expansion plans on hold and fight for its survival.

One 'boom' area of the air transport industry in the early 2000s was the low-cost airline market. Easyjet and Ryanair had been successful from the start, and when the British Airways low-cost subsidiary Go announced plans to open services out of its East Midlands base, bmi was forced to react by setting up its own budget airline there. Two months after the announcement of its formation in

January 2002, the bmi subsidiary, bmibaby, became operational using two Boeing 737 srs 500s and a Fokker 70 transferred across from the bmi and bmi Regional fleets. The inaugural bmibaby service departed East Midlands for Malaga on 20 March 2002, and, in October of that year, bmi announced that it would be transferring all of its scheduled service routes out of East Midlands to its low-cost subsidiary. After a successful first season, bmibaby bases were established at many other UK airports and the fleet was expanded to eventually include 28 Boeing 737 srs 300s and srs 500s.

Meanwhile, on the transatlantic front, the Manchester–Chicago route had proved to be an almost instant success, but this was not the case with the service to Washington DC. Part of the trouble was its awkward arrival time into Washington DC, which was too late in the day to make good onward connections across the US. Demand slumped during the winter of 2003–04, and the service was temporarily suspended. To maintain its utilisation, the A330 allocated was used on a four-month Ministry of

Left: Fokker 100 G-BVJA on stand at Edinburgh in 1996 wearing 'British Midland–The Airline for Europe' titles. (Graham Marchbank)

Below: Fokker 100 G-BVJA on pushback in 1998. (Eric Melrose)

Saab 340A G-GNTF was formerly with Aberdeen-based Business Air. (Rob Hodgkins)

Saab 340B G-GNTI at Paris (Charles de Gaulle) in 1997. (Denis Deparis)

Above: Saab 340A G-GNTD with British Midland Commuter titles, at Edinburgh in 1993. (Graham Marchbank)

Left: Saab 340A G-GNTF, a former Business Air machine, at Glasgow in 1998. (Eric Melrose)

Defence contract to transport military personnel from RAF Brize Norton to Ascension Island and the Falklands, the aircraft wearing Star Alliance livery. The Washington DC route was relaunched in March 2005 but again failed to attract the hoped-for passenger figures. The A330 was transferred onto new services to Mumbai and Delhi and replaced on the Washington DC route by a smaller, leased-in Boeing 757. This single-aisle jet did not appeal to transatlantic travellers, and the Washington DC route was finally terminated on 30 October 2005. In March 2004, bmi announced that, from April, an A330 aircraft would operate services between Manchester and Toronto, and, from November 2004, the airline would operate winter-sun flights from Manchester to Barbados, Antigua and St Lucia, while still keeping a reduced winter flight frequency to the US in the shape of Manchester–Las Vegas services from 31 October 2004. In spite of the setbacks, bmi remained the UK's second-largest full-service air carrier, operating to 29 destinations. In 2003, Lufthansa had increased its stake in bmi to 30 per cent minus one share, with the three founders of British Midland Holdings still holding 50 per cent plus

Jetstream 41 G-MAJA was leased from Manx Airlines during 1994–96 and is seen here at Paris (CDG). (Denis Deparis)

one share. In 2004, an overhaul of the domestic and European routes out of Heathrow was carried out, under the name of the New Business Model. Apart from the services to the key destinations of Edinburgh, Glasgow, Belfast, Dublin and Brussels, all routes were to become all-Economy. Many were suspended, to be replaced in the coming years by new ones with more potential, and the A320 and A321 aircraft were to be replaced by 144-seat Airbus A319s as their leases expired.

In 2005, bmi became the designated UK carrier for services to Saudi Arabia. A330 flights to Riyadh commenced on 1 September 2005, followed by services to Jeddah from 18 May 2006. On 20 May 2006, Stuart Balmforth and John Wolfe ended their partnership in the airline and retired. Michael Bishop acquired their shares, leaving him with a personal stake of 50 per cent plus one share. On 29 October 2006, another new destination came online when bmi, operating in conjunction with the Russian carrier Transaero, inaugurated Heathrow–Moscow services using a dedicated A320 aircraft fitted with special leather seats at a 40-inch pitch. It was during this month, however, that the Heathrow–Mumbai service came to an end. This promising route had been inaugurated on 14 May 2005, and the service had later been upgraded to a daily frequency, but, after more than a year of promising operations, stress fractures in the undercarriage of the A330 allocated to the route forced the withdrawal of the aircraft for repairs. These eventually took around three months to complete, and, in the meantime, market share had been irreplaceably lost to competitors. Bmi survived all these setbacks, and, in February 2007, took over the UK airline BMed (formerly known as British Mediterranean Airways). This carrier had built up a network of services to destinations in Africa, the Middle East and the Commonwealth of Independent States, in the former USSR. It had been operating as a British Airways franchisee since 1997, but had been struggling financially after soaring oil prices, the loss of its successful Heathrow–Beirut route and the withdrawal of support by its biggest backer. Bmi's successful £30m bid for the airline added 17 new destinations to its route map, along with eight more Airbus A321 jets. The first former BMed service to be operated as a bmi flight departed Heathrow for Baku, Azerbaijan, on 28 October 2007. Once the BMed franchise agreement with British Airways had expired, the former BMed aircraft were repainted in a modified bmi livery.

Airbus A321 G-MIDA tucks up its undercarriage after take-off from Edinburgh. (Gerry Hill)

Above: Former British Mediterranean Airbus A321 G-MEDL on tow at Heathrow. (Graham Marchbank)

Below: Airbus A321 G-MIDC taxiing out at Heathrow. (Graham Marchbank)

Airbus A320 G-MIDX in Star Alliance livery at Heathrow. (Eric Melrose)

Above: Bmi Airbus A320 G-MIDV at Heathrow. (Eric Melrose)

Below: Airbus A321 G-MIDK climbs out from Manchester. (Eric Melrose)

Bmi Airbus A320 G-MIDP at Heathrow. (Eric Melrose)

Above: Airbus A321 G-MIDM at Heathrow. (Eric Melrose)

Below: A taxiing shot of Airbus G-MIDU at Heathrow. (Eric Melrose)

Airbus A320 G-MIDT with 'British Midland-bmi' titles at Heathrow. (Eric Melrose)

Above: Airbus A320 G-MIDO at Heathrow. (Eric Melrose)

Below: Embraer 145 G-RJXE with 'British Midland-bmi' titles at Edinburgh. (Eric Melrose)

An unusual location for Embraer 145 G-RJXE, seen here at Stornoway. (Eric Melrose)

Above: Embraer 145 G-RJXD on climb-out from Edinburgh. (Eric Melrose)

Below: Embraer 145 G-RJXD at Aberdeen. (Eric Melrose)

Airbus A330 G-WWBD in Star Alliance livery at Manchester on a transatlantic schedule in 2004. (Eric Melrose)

Above: Airbus A330 G-WWBM in bmi livery at Manchester in 2007. (Eric Melrose)

Below: Airbus A330 G-WWBB at Manchester in 2007. (Eric Melrose)

Boeing 757 srs 200 TF-FII was leased from Icelandair for transatlantic services and is seen at Manchester in 2005. (Eric Melrose)

Above: Bmibaby began low-cost services in March 2002. Among its large fleet of Boeing 737s was srs 500 G-BVZI. (Eric Melrose)

Below: Bmibaby Boeing 737 srs 300 G-TOYE at Manchester in July 2007. (Eric Melrose)

Above and below: Fokker 70 G-BVTF at Edinburgh in 1998. (Author)

Fokker 100 PH-CFE is seen at Edinburgh in 1996 whilst on lease from the maker. It later became G-BXWE. (Author)

Saab 340B G-GNTI at Aberdeen in 1997. (Author)

Above: Embraer 145 G-RJXC taxies in at Aberdeen in 2000. (Author)

Below: Embraer 145 G-RJXC comes onto its stand at Aberdeen in 2000. (Author)

Embraer 145 G-RJXB in 'Diamond' livery at Aberdeen. (Author)

Above: Embraer 135 G-RJXJ at Aberdeen in 2003. (Author)

Below: Airbus A320 G-MIDS on approach to Edinburgh in 2003. (Author)

Airbus A320 G-MIDO at Aberdeen in 2005. (Author)

Above left: Airbus A320 G-MIDO at Aberdeen in 2005. (Author)

Above right: Cover of a brochure describing bmi's forthcoming North Atlantic services out of Manchester. (via Author)

Chapter 7

Towards the End

Bmi added another Middle East destination to its portfolio the following year when Heathrow–Tel Aviv services were inaugurated on 14 March 2008. More wide-bodied A330s were needed, but until they could be sourced and placed into service, two Boeing 757s were leased from Astraeus, initially for two years. These were used to increase capacity on the former BMed services to Almaty and Freetown and on the Tel Aviv route. On 15 November 2008, bmi announced that it would be terminating all of its long-haul operations out of Manchester in the spring of 2009 and transferring the two A330s based there to Heathrow for use on services to Cairo and Amman. During 2008, the news emerged that Lufthansa had agreed to buy out Michael Bishop's 50 per cent shareholding in bmi in 2009, thereby raising its own stake in the carrier to 80 per cent. The 2008 stock market upheavals prompted Lufthansa to try to back out of the deal, but Bishop threatened to sue if they did. Lufthansa eventually settled out of court for a reported £223m and its shareholding was duly increased. In 2009, Lufthansa announced a restructuring of both bmi and bmi Regional in an effort to stem the losses of these carriers by adjusting capacity. Nine aircraft, including two operated by bmi Regional, were to

Airbus A319 G-DBCB at Heathrow in 2005. (Eric Melrose)

Airbus A320 G-MIDY at Moscow (DME) airport on a service from Heathrow in July 2007. (Eric Melrose)

be disposed of and the routes linking Heathrow to Amsterdam, Brussels, Tel Aviv, Kiev and Aleppo were to be suspended at the start of the 2010 summer season. The frequency of the services from Heathrow to Aberdeen, Belfast, Dublin, Edinburgh, Glasgow and Manchester were to be scaled back, hopefully improving the yields on these routes, and freeing up Heathrow slots for sale or re-use within the Lufthansa group. The remaining premium class cabins on domestic routes were to be removed and 600 staff were to be made redundant. By 2010, bmi Regional had acquired a fleet of 18 Embraer 145 and 135 regional jets. Three of these were contracted out to mainline bmi, two were carrying out a long-term contract with Airbus for staff shuttle services between manufacturing centres, and a further two were operating services for Brussels Airlines. From April 2010, the airline began using the British Midland International name on Middle East routes, as passengers from this area had not really connected with the bmi name and were more likely to choose an airline with the word 'British' in its title. The bmi name and logo were, however, retained for use in the domestic market. In January 2011, bmi announced that Heathrow–Glasgow services would cease from 27 March that year. The airline had been operating up to seven flights daily over this route in competition with British Airways but was losing £1m each month by doing so. The slots and aircraft freed up would be redeployed and used on new routes from Heathrow to Bergen, Stavanger, Casablanca and Marrakesh. Lufthansa would use bmi A320s on three times-daily Lufthansa services to Frankfurt from Birmingham and Manchester. None of these measures proved sufficient to stem the continuing losses, and, in September 2011, Lufthansa announced that it was putting bmi up for sale. In early November, the International Airline Group (IAG), the parent company of British Airways, Iberia and other carriers, announced that it had reached agreement in principle on the purchase of bmi from Lufthansa. A month later, Virgin Atlantic Airways made a counteroffer, but, by 22 December 2011, IAG had entered into a contractual agreement to buy bmi for £172.5m. The deal gave Lufthansa the option to sell off bmibaby and bmi Regional separately, as IAG was not interested in acquiring these subsidiaries if another buyer could be found. On 30 March 2012, the EEC approved the sale, subject to IAG giving up 14 of its members airlines' daily slots at Heathrow. Twenty days later, ownership was transferred. On 10 May 2012, IAG announced the sale of bmi Regional to the Aberdeen-based Sector Aviation holdings consortium for around £8m. Bmibaby continued operating under IAG ownership for a while but was under constant threat of closure unless a buyer could be found. None was forthcoming, and, on 9 September 2012, the low-cost airline ceased trading. The final service under the bmi name was operated from Baku to Heathrow on 27 October 2012 by Airbus A321 G-MEDF. As was the case with most significant flights into the airport, its arrival was greeted by a water-cannon salute provided by the airport fire service.

Airbus A320 G-MIDY at Belfast City Airport in March 2007. (Eric Melrose)

Above: Airbus A319
DBCK on take-off
from Aberdeen
in March 2007.
(Eric Melrose)

Right: Airbus A321
G-MIDL in Star
Alliance livery at
Heathrow in 2007.
(Eric Melrose)

Below: Airbus A319
G-DBCA at Heathrow
in 2005. (Eric Melrose)

Embraer 145 G-RJXB on tow at Aberdeen in June 2006. (Eric Melrose)

Above: Airbus A319 G-DBCH at a wintry Heathrow in February 2009. (Eric Melrose)

Below: Airbus A321 G-MEDF operated the final bmi service in October 2012. Seen here at Heathrow in February 2009. (Eric Melrose)

Above: Airbus A321 G-MIDL wears the slogan 'Ten Years 1997–2007', along with the Star Alliance livery, at Manchester in July 2007. (Eric Melrose)

Right: A close-up of Airbus A319 G-DBCE taxiing at Edinburgh in 2011. (Gerry Hill)

Former BMed Airbus A320 G-MEDE in an interim livery at Edinburgh in 2009. (Gerry Hill)

Above: Embraer 135 G-RJXK in Star Alliance livery at Aberdeen in June 2003. (Author)

Left: Embraer 135 G-RJXK in bmi livery at Manchester in September 2013. (Author)

Below: Embraer 145 G-EMBI, in a white livery with bmi Regional titles at Aberdeen in July 2014, was formerly operated by British Regional Airlines. (Author)

Fleet Lists

NB Many aircraft were leased and sub-leased between British Midland and subsidiary companies, Manx Airlines and Loganair.

The dates of acquisition, lease and return, or sale, are all as shown on the UK Civil Aviation Authority G-INFO website.

The 'date acquired' refers to the date the aircraft was registered to the company, not necessarily the date it was delivered.

1. Fleet list of aircraft operated by Derby Airways (including Wolverhampton Aviation and Air Schools), British Midland Airways and mainline bmi.

Abbreviations used: lsd=leased; wfu=withdrawn from use; dbr=damaged beyond repair; re-regd=re-registered; Transf=transferred; BRAL=British Regional Air Lines; BA=British Airways; BMA=British Midland

Aircraft type	Constructors No	Registration	Date acquired	Fate
DH 85 Leopard	7028	G-ACLL	30 July 1959	Transf to BMA; Sold May 1971
DH 89A Dragon Rapide	6325	G-AEAL	20 March 1953	Sold 22 November 1955
	6640	G-AIUK	18 June 1948	Sold 14 February 1955
	6837	G-AIUL	9 June 1954	Sold 11 March 1957
	6767	G-AKME	21 February 1950	Written off 30 June 1950
	6612	G-AKOV	9 August 1950	Sold 7 February 1955
	6907	G-ALGE	6 May 1952	Sold 29 May 1954
Miles M38 Messenger 2A	6341	G-AILL	4 February 1947	Sold 29 May 1953
Miles M65 Gemini 1A	6465	G-AJZJ	18 June 1948	Sold 2 August 1957
Miles M57 Aerovan 4	6420	G-AJZN	18 June 1948	Sold 18 May 1951
DH 104 Dove 5	04474	G-AROI	21 November 1961	Sold 19 November 1963
Handley Page HPR1 Marathon 1	115	G-AMET	28 April 1959	Withdrawn 23 October 1959
	118	G-AMEW	16 August 1957	Withdrawn 27 September 1960
	127	G-AMGW	11 October 1955	Withdrawn 25 July 1960
	129	G-AMHR	11 October 1955	Withdrawn 18 July 1960

Aircraft type	Constructors No	Registration	Date acquired	Fate
Douglas C-47 Dakota 3	13164	G-AKJH	20 April 1961	Sold March 1969
	14969	G-ANTD	27 April 1955	Sold October 1968
Douglas C-47 Dakota 4	12195	G-AGJV	13 December 1960	Sold March 1969
	9131	G-AOFZ	5 February 1960	Sold April 1966
	16171	G-AMSW	31 December 1958	Crashed 7 October 1961
	16448	G-AMSX	31 December 1958	Sold January 1966
	16534	G-AOGZ	18 February 1956	Sold April 1967
	15676	G-APBC	2 May 1958	Sold April 1968
Canadair C-4	153	G-ALHG	14 November 1961	Crashed 4 June 1967
	160	G-ALHN	16 November 1961	Broken up for spares
	162	G-ALHP	16 November 1961	Broken up for spares
	164	G-ALHS	14 November 1961	Withdrawn May 1970
	167	G-ALHV	December 1963	Broken up for spares
	170	G-ALHY	14 November 1961	Withdrawn May 1970
Handley Page Herald	161	G-ASKK	1 February 1965	Sold December 1967
	165	G-ATHE	August 1965	September 1965 (on loan from HP)
	149	G-APWA	April 1966	September 1966 (on loan from HP)
	185	G-ASVO	9 March 1973	Sold January 1977
	177	G-ATIG	18 April 1973	Sold January 1977
	194	G-BAVX	18 April 1973	Sold January 1977
Vickers V.702 Viscount	073	G-APPX	4 April 1969	Lsd until October 1969
Vickers V.736 Viscount	077	G-AODG	January 1967	Dbr 20 February 1969
Vickers V.755 Viscount	092	G-AOCB	11 February 1969	Wfu October 1969
	093	G-AOCC	11 February 1969	Wfu April 1969
Vickers V.760 Viscount	186	G-AWCV	7 April 1968	Wfu April 1970
Vickers V.785 Viscount	116	G-AWGV	12 April 1968	Wfu April 1970
Vickers V.813 Viscount	346	G-AZLP	4 January 1972	Wfu November 1983
	347	G-AZLR	4 January 1972	Wfu June 1983
	348	G-AZLS	4 January 1972	Wfu March 1982
	349	G-AZLT/ G-BMAT	4 January 1972	Re-regd 30 March 1981; sold October 1987
	350	G-AZNA	8 February 1972	Sold August 1988
	351	G-AZNB	8 February 1972	Sold May 1986
	352	G-AZNC	8 February 1972	Wfu February 1982

Aircraft type	Constructors No	Registration	Date acquired	Fate
Vickers V.814 Viscount	338	G-BAPF	February 1972–October 1975 and May 1978–May 1986	Sold May 1986
	339	G-AWXI	21 January 1969	Dbr 22 January 1970
	340	G-BAPD	February 1972–September 1975 and October 1977–September 1978	Wfu September 1978
	341	G-BAPE	February 1972	Sold October 1977
	344	G-BAPG	February 1973	Sold January 1978
	370	G-AYOX	1 April 1978	Wfu January 1984
Vickers V.815 Viscount	336	G-AVJA	2 June 1967 (lsd)	Dbr 20 March 1969
	375	G-AVJB	3 June 1967 (lsd); bought March 1972	Sold December 1976
Vickers V.831 Viscount	402	G-APND	January 1969 (lsd); bought February 1973	Sold November 1973
	403	G-APNE	March 1967 (lsd); bought October 1971	Sold September 1972
	419	G ASED	February 1967 (lsd until March 1972)	
Vickers V.833 Viscount	426	G-APTD	20 April 1969	Sold February 1970
Vickers V.836 Viscount	435	G-BFZL	12 March 1979	Sold December 1988
Vickers V.838 Viscount	446	G-BCZR	(Lsd) May–October 1976 and May–October 1977	
BAC One-Eleven srs 523FJ	193	G-AXLL	29 July 1969	Sold May 1973
	199	G-AXLM	29 July 1969	Sold April 1974
	211	G-AXLN	29 July 1969	Sold November 1973
BAC One-Eleven srs 304AX	112	G-WLAD	Lsd from Airways International Cymru October 1985–March 1987	
Boeing 707 srs 321	17597	G-AYBJ	4 March 1970	Wfu December 1977
	17598	G-AYVG	December 1974	Sold July 1980
	18083	G-AYVE	31 December 1970	Sold January 1978
	17605	G-AZWA	20 May 1975	Sold October 1977
	17608	G-AYXR	Lsd July 1975; bought September 1975	Sold April 1980

Aircraft type	Constructors No	Registration	Date acquired	Fate
Boeing 707 srs 321C	19270	N448M/ G-BMAZ	March 1979; re-regd May 1982	Sold September 1985
Boeing 707 srs 321F	17602	G-BAEL	March 1975	Sold June 1978
Boeing 707 srs 324C	18886	G-AZJM	Lsd 25 May 1977–December 1980	
Boeing 707 srs 338C	19625	G-BFLD	Lsd 16 March 1978–October 1984	
	19293	G-BFLE	Lsd 17 May 1978–November 1984	
Boeing 707 srs 373C	19442	N370WA	Lsd 15 August 1977–December 1978	
Fokker F-27 Friendship	10106	G-IOMA	20 September 1972	Sold April 1986 (lsd to Manx 1982–83 and 1983–86)
	10256	PH-KFH/ G-BMAE	Lsd 26 October 1981	Sold November 1988; bought 1 November 1982; re-regd 9 November 1982
	10227	G-BMAS	Lsd 8 October 1981–May 1983	
	10225	G-BAUR	Lsd 8 January 1984 and 15 February– 28 September 1984	
	10231	G-BLGW	Lsd 1 March 1982–31 March 1985	
	10289	G-BDDH	Lsd 1 April 1982–16 February 1984	
	10302	G-BMAP	29 January 1982	Sold 17 November 1988 (lsd to Loganair and Manx)
	10229	G-BHMW	Lsd 19 December 1982–2 October 1983	
	10212	G-BMAW	6 September 1983	Sold 2 November 1988
	10241	G-BMAU	1 January 1983	Dbr 18 January 1987
Douglas DC-9 srs 14	45712	OH-LYB	Lsd June 1983–December 1995 (re-regd as G-BMAH)	
	45713	G-BMAI	September 1983	Sold April 1995
Douglas DC-9 srs 15	47048	G-BFIH/ G-BMAA	April 1978	Re-regd March 1980; sold March 1993
	45723	N48075	Lsd February– September 1978	

Aircraft type	Constructors No	Registration	Date acquired	Fate
	45738	G-BMAB	Lsd November 1979–September 1994	
	45739	G-BMAC	February 1980	Sold April 1982
			December 1982	Sold August 1995
	45719	G-BMAG	February 1983	Sold April 1995
Douglas DC-9 srs 32	47430	G-BMAK	Lsd January 1984–December 1994	
	47468	G-BMAM	Lsd January 1984–December 1994	
	47570	G-BMWD	Lsd November 1988–April 1990	
	47648	G-PKBM	Lsd January 1987–June 1995	
	47666	G-PKBD	Lsd August 1988–January 1995	
	47484	G-ELDG	April 1990	Sold May 1996
	47555	G-ELDH	May 1990	Sold February 1996
	47559	G-ELDI	May 1990	Sold March 1996
	47523	G-PKBE	Lsd October 1988–December 1994	
Shorts 330	SH.3077	G-BJFK	Lsd September 1983–May 1984	
Shorts 360	SH.3608	G-BKMX	Lsd May 1983	Transf to BRAL January 1997
	SH.3611	G-BMAJ/ G-WACK	Lsd May 1983	Re-regd April 1986; Transf to BRAL January 1997
	SH.3633	G-BMAR	Lsd August 1984–January 1987	
	SH.3688	G-BMLC	Lsd April 1986–April 1990	
	SH.3686	G-BMHX	Lsd April 1986–June 1990	
	SH.3687	G-BMHY	Lsd April 1986–September 1988	
Jetstream 41	41032	G-MAJA	Lsd May 1994–September 1996	
British Aerospace ATP	2003	G-BMYK	Lsd July 1989–December 1993	
	2004	G-BMYL	Lsd July 1989–October 1991	
	2002	G-BMYM	Lsd July 1989–December 1993	

Aircraft type	Constructors No	Registration	Date acquired	Fate
De Havilland DH104 Dove 5	04474	G-AROI	November 1961	Sold November 1963
De Havilland Canada DHC-7	110	G-BOAW	Lsd July 1991–March 1994 and April–June 1995	
	112	G-BOAY	July 1991	Sold November 1995
Boeing 737 srs 200	21735	EI-BTR	Lsd May–December 1988	
	21231	OO-THE	Lsd March–June 1988	
	21719	OO-TEK	Lsd October–November 1986	
Boeing 737 srs 300	23831	G-OBMA	Lsd October 1987–November 1993	
	23832	G-OBMB	Lsd October 1987–December 1993	
	24030	G-OBMC	Lsd January 1989–January 1994	
	24092	G-OBMD	Lsd February 1989–December 1998	
	24460	G-OBMH	Lsd March 1990–March 2001	
	24461	G-OBMJ	Lsd March 1990–December 2000	
	24300	G-OBML	Lsd November 1991–May 1997	
	24963	G-OBMP	Lsd January 1992	Transf to BA October 2012
	28537	G-ODSK	Lsd July 1997	Transf to BA October 2012
	28558	G-OJTW	Lsd April 1997–June 2005	
	28557	G-SMDB	Lsd March 1997	Transf to BA October 2012
	24962	G-BYZJ	Lsd January 2000–February 2009	
	28554	G-ECAS	Lsd December 1996–June 2005	
Boeing 737 srs 400	23867	G-OBME	Lsd October 1988	Destroyed January 1989
	23868	G-OBMF	Lsd October 1988–December 2000	
	23870	G-OBMG	Lsd March 1989–March 1999	
	25596	G-OBMK	Lsd April 1992–April 1997	

Aircraft type	Constructors No	Registration	Date acquired	Fate
	25177	G-OBMM	Lsd December 1991–April 2003	
	26280	G-OBMO	Lsd March 1992–May 2000	
	28723	G-SFBH	Lsd May 1997–May 2002	
	24123	G-BOPJ/ G-OBMN	Lsd May 1990–December 1997 (re-regd November 1991)	
Boeing 737 srs 500	24694	G-BVKA	Lsd February 1994–April 2004	
	27268	G-BVKB	Lsd March 1994	Transf to BA October 2012
	24695	G-BVKC	Lsd April 1994–June 2004	
	26421	G-BVKD	Lsd November 1994–April 2011	
	26422	G-BVZE	Lsd March 1995	Transf to BA October 2012
	25038	G-BVZF	Lsd April 1995	Transf to BA February 2000
	25160	G-BVZG	Lsd April 1995–March 2008	
	25166	G-BVZH	Lsd April 1995–December 2007	
	25167	G-BVZI	Lsd May 1995–May 2008	
	25185	G-OBMR	Lsd May 1996–November 2000	
	25065	G-OBMX	Lsd September 1993–March 2001	
	26419	G-OBMY	Lsd September 1993–September 1998	
	24754	G-OBMZ	Lsd September 1993–January 2001	
Boeing 757 srs 200	24760	TF-FII	Lsd May–October 2005	
	25621	G-STRX	Lsd May–December 2008	
	28161	G-STRY	Lsd March 2008–June 2011	
Boeing 767 srs 300	27619	PH-MCV	Lsd September–October 2007	

Aircraft type	Constructors No	Registration	Date acquired	Fate
Fokker 70	11538	G-BVTE	Lsd April 1995–February 2002	
	11539	G-BVTF	Lsd May 1995–October 2002	
	11551	G-BVTG	Lsd September 1995–April 2002	
Fokker 100	11489	G-BVJA	Lsd April 1994–April 2004	
	11488	G-BVJB	Lsd July 1994–August 2004	
	11497	G-BVJC	Lsd December 1994–February 2005	
	11503	G-BVJD	Lsd December 1994–March 2005	
	11327	G-BXWE	Lsd May 1996; bought July 1998	Sold July 2005
	11328	G-BXWF	Lsd April 1996; bought July 1998	Sold April 2005
Airbus A319-131	2098	G-DBCA	Lsd February 2004	Transf to BA December 2012
	2188	G-DBCB	Lsd April 2004	Transf to BA May 2012
	2194	G-DBCC	Lsd May 2004	Transf to BA June 2012
	2389	G-DBCD	Lsd February 2005	Transf to BA June 2012
	2429	G-DBCE	Lsd March 2005	Transf to BA July 2012
	2466	G-DBCF	Lsd May 2005	Transf to BA July 2012
	2694	G-DBCG	Lsd February 2006	Transf to BA July 2012
	2697	G-DBCH	Lsd February 2006	Transf to BA June 2012
	2720	G-DBCI	Lsd May 2006	Transf to BA August 2012
	2981	G-DBCJ	Lsd January 2007	Transf to BA August 2012
	3049	G-DBCK	Lsd March 2007	Transf to BA August 2012
Airbus A320-232	1922	G-MEDH	Lsd December 2007	Transf to BA November 2012
	2441	G-MEDK	Lsd December 2007	Transf to BA May 2013
	1987	G-MIDO	Lsd April 2003	Transf to BA February 2013
	1424	G-MIDS	Lsd March 2001	Transf to BA September 2012
	1418	G-MIDT	Lsd March 2001	Transf to BA September 2012
	1177	G-MIDX	Lsd March 2000	Transf to BA December 2012

Aircraft type	Constructors No	Registration	Date acquired	Fate
	1014	G-MIDY	Lsd June 1999	Transf to BA October 2012
	1407	G-MIDU	Lsd February 2001	Sold April 2008
	1383	G-MIDV	Lsd January 2001	Sold February 2008
	1183	G-MIDW	Lsd March 2000	Sold April 2007
	934	G-MIDZ	Lsd January 1999	Sold March 2009
	1697	G-MIDR	Lsd April 2002	Sold June 2010
	1732	G-MIDP	Lsd May 2002	Sold July 2010
	1194	G-MEDE	Lsd November 2007	Sold May 2010
Airbus A321-231	1690	G-MEDF	Lsd December 2007	Transf to BA December 2012
	1711	G-MEDG	Lsd November 2007	Transf to BA December 2012
	2190	G-MEDJ	Lsd December 2007	Transf to BA May 2013
	2653	G-MEDL	Lsd November 2007	Transf to BA November 2012
	2799	G-MEDM	Lsd November 2007	Transf to BA October 2012
	3512	G-MEDN	Lsd May 2008	Transf to BA October 2012
	3926	G-MEDU	Lsd July 2009	Transf to BA November 2012
	806	G-MIDA	Lsd March 1998	Sold April 2005
	835	G-MIDC	Lsd June 1998	Sold November 2010
	864	G-MIDE	Lsd August 1998	Sold May 2006
	810	G-MIDF	Lsd April 1998	Sold April 2005
	968	G-MIDH	Lsd March 1999	Sold March 2006
	974	G-MIDI	Lsd March 1999	Sold April 2006
	1045	G-MIDJ	Lsd July 1999	Sold January 2007
	1153	G-MIDK	Lsd January 2000	Sold April 2007
	1174	G-MIDL	Lsd February 2000	Sold September 2010
	1207	G-MIDM	Lsd April 2000	Sold May 2007
Airbus A330-243	401	G-WWBD	Lsd May 2001	Sold February 2013
	398	G-WWBM	Lsd April	Sold October 2013
	404	G-WWBB	Lsd May 2001	Sold July 2010

British Midland used many general aviation types for company transport, crew-ferrying, etc. SIAI SF-260 G-BAGB is seen here at Denham in January 2008. (Glyn Charles Jones)

Aircraft type	Constructors No	Registration	Date acquired	Fate
Aircraft operated by British Midland Commuter/British Midland Regional				
(NB Many of this subsidiary's aircraft were transferred from the mainline company, and several of its aircraft were operated on the mainline company's routes under contract.)				
Saab 340	340A-100	G-GNTD	Lsd December 1992–March 2001	
	340A-133	G-GNTE	Lsd January 1993–August 2001	
	340A-113	G-GNTF	Lsd October 1994–March 2001	
	340A-126	G-GNTG	Lsd November 1994–April 2001	
	340B-169	G-GNTH	Lsd January 1997–September 2001	
	340B-172	G-GNTI	Lsd January 1997–August 2001	
	340B-192	G-GNTJ	Lsd February 1997–November 2001	

Aircraft type	Constructors No	Registration	Date acquired	Fate
BAe 146-200	E2024	G-CLHA	Lsd March 2000–May 2002	
	E2036	G-CLHB	Lsd March 2000–February 2002	
	E2088	G-CLHC	Lsd May 2000–February 2002	
	E2023	G-CLHD	Lsd May 2000–October 2003	
	E2045	G-CLHE	Lsd September 2000–March 2002	
Embraer 145	145136	G-RJXA	Lsd June 2012–March 2019	
	145142	G-RJXB	Lsd June 2012–March 2019	
	145153	G-RJXC	Lsd June 2012–February 2019	
	145207	G-RJXD	Lsd June 2012–February 2019	
	145245	G-RJXE	Lsd June 2012–February 2019	
	145280	G-RJXF	Lsd June 2012–December 2018	
	145390	G-RJXG	Lsd June 2012–April 2019	
	145442	G-RJXH	Lsd June 2012–February 2019	
	145454	G-RJXI	Lsd June 2012–February 2019	
	145216	G-RJXM	Lsd June 2012–February 2019	
	145336	G-RJXN	Lsd November 2006–November 2009	
	145339	G-RJXO	Lsd October 2006–February 2010	
	145070	SE-DZA	Lsd February–June 2001	
	145070	G-CCYH/ G-RJXR	Lsd February 2005; re-regd April 2008	Sold August 2018
	145036	CS-TPJ	Lsd March 2003–March 2004	
	145113	SE-DZB	Lsd May–November 2000	

Aircraft type	Constructors No	Registration	Date acquired	Fate
Embraer 135	145473	G-RJXJ	Lsd June 2012–October 2018	
	145494	G-RJXK	Lsd June 2012–March 2019	
	145376	G-RJXL	Lsd June 2012–March 2019	
	145210	SE-RAA	Lsd March 2003–March 2004	
	145431	G-CDFS	Lsd June 2012–March 2019	
Aircraft operated by bmibaby (actually registered to mainline bmi)				
Boeing 737 srs 300	24963	G-OBMP	Lsd January 1992–October 2013	
	28554	G-ECAS	Lsd December 1996–June 2005	
	28557	G-SMDB/ G-TOYF	Lsd as G-SMDB March 1997–March 2002 and as G-TOYF December 2005–November 2013	
	28558	G-OJTW	Lsd April 1997–June 2005	
	28537	G-ODSK	Lsd July 1997–December 2013	
	24962	G-BYZJ	Lsd January 2000–February 2009	
	27833	G-OGBD	Lsd April 2004–June 2013	
	27834	G-OGBE	Lsd May 2004–April 2009	
	26310	G-TOYA	Lsd December 2004–May 2010	
	26311	G-TOYB	Lsd November 2004–May 2010	
	26312	G-TOYC	Lsd December 2004–May 2010	
	26307	G-TOYD	Lsd June 2005–November 2014	
	27455	G-TOYE	Lsd May 2005–June 2009	
	28872	G-TOYG	Lsd January 2006–November 2014	

Bmibaby Boeing 737 srs 500 G-BVZG at Manchester in July 2005. (Eric Melrose)

Aircraft type	Constructors No	Registration	Date acquired	Fate
	28570	G-TOYH	Lsd December 2005–November 2013	
	28054	G-TOYI	Lsd July 2008–September 2014	
	28332	G-TOYJ	Lsd April 2007–July 2013	
	28870	G-TOYK	Lsd May 2007–September 2013	
	29141	G-TOYM	Lsd August 2008–May 2013	
Boeing 737 srs 500	27268	G-BVKB	Lsd March 1994–July 2013	
	24695	G-BVKC	Lsd May 1994–June 2004	
	26421	G-BVKD	Lsd November 1994–April 2011	
	25160	G-BVZG	Lsd April 1995–March 2008	
	25166	G-BVZH	Lsd April 1995–December 2007	
Miscellaneous aircraft used by British Midland for communications duties, etc.				
SIAI-Marchetti SF260	107	G-BAGB	January 1979	Sold June 2010
Beech 58 Baron	TH-293	G-BAHN	April 1981	Sold January 1988

Bibliography

Many sources, digital and otherwise, have been consulted during the process.

Books

Austen, Michael, et al, *Jet Airliners of the World 1949–1998*, Air-Britain (Historians) Ltd. (1998)

Cowell, G, *Handley Page Herald*, Janes, Northampton (1980)

Cramp, B G, *British Midland Airways*, Airline Publications and Sales (1979)

Ginsberg, Malcolm, *London City Airport: Thirty Years Serving The Capital*, Business Travel News Ltd (2017)

Gunston, Bill, *Diamond Flight: The Story of British Midland*, Henry Melland Ltd (1988)

Halford-MacLeod, Guy, *Britain's Airlines: Volume One: 1946–1951*, The History Press, Cheltenham (2006)

Halford-MacLeod, Guy, *Britain's Airlines: Volume Two: 1951–1964*, The History Press, Cheltenham (2007)

Halford-MacLeod, Guy, *Britain's Airlines: Volume Three: 1964 to Deregulation*, The History Press, Cheltenham (2010)

Hutchison, Iain, *The Story of Loganair: Scotland's Airline – The First 25 Years*, Western Isles Publishing (1987)

Merton-Jones, A C, *British Independent Airlines: 1946–1976*, The Aviation Hobby Shop, Middlesex (2000)

Olsen, Penny, *Bmi the Story: Celebrating 70 Years in the Business of Aviation* Granta Editions, London (2008)

Magazines

Various issues of:
   Air-Britain Aviation World, Air-Britain Trust Ltd
   Aircraft Illustrated, Ian Allen Publishing
   Airliner Classics, Key Publishing Ltd
   Airliner World, Key Publishing Ltd
   Propliner Aviation Magazine

Websites

The UK Civil Aviation Authority G-INFO database, http://www.caa.gov.uk/Aircraft-register/G-INFO

The UK Government Air Accident Investigation Board reports website, https://www.gov.uk/aaib-reports